Six weeks' holiday

True stories about the myths
and realities of working in Sweden

Joshua Bookman

Catherine Derieux

Kateřina Duchoňová

Nausherwan Ghaffar

Marco Guadarrama

Clarissa Hirst

Jill Leckie

Franziska Müller

Veronika Opatřilová

Raman Ramalingam

Morag Ramsey

Werner Renck

Adriana Salazar

Maddy Savage

Olga Talalay

Federica Viero

Angeliki Vlachou

Thanks to
Sarah and Joanne, who made this project possible.

LYS läromedel | PYS validering AB
Editorial office: redaktion@lysforlag.com
www.lysforlag.com
Creative Editor: Sofi Tegsveden Deveaux
Cover design: Sofi Tegsveden Deveaux
LYS | LÄROMEDEL I YRKESSVENSKA

International Edition
© 2018 The co-authors, Sofi Tegsveden Deveaux
& LYS läromedel   978-91-984715-9-5

Six weeks' holiday

True stories about the myths
and realities of working in Sweden

Ed. Sofi Tegsveden Deveaux

Contents

Introduction by the editor   11
Sofi Tegsveden Deveaux

Glossary   18

1. Why write? _____
Flush   24
Kateřina Duchoňova
Not a Swedish class   34
Morag Ramsey
A recipe for a successful work life in Sweden   44
Adriana Salazar

2. Leap _____
You are the hero of this story   60
Catherine Derieux
Home   76
Clarissa Hirst
Some reverse American dreams   90
Joshua Bookman

3. Expectations _____
Me, a feminist, too   102
Maddy Savage
Mother of all let downs   110
Jill Leckie

4. Eyes of others _____
Subject: (No subject) 126
Franziska Müller
Trust score 140
Raman Ramalingam
The fourth reflection or the broken mirror 144
Werner Renck

5.Making sense _____
Naked so what 154
Federica Viero
Untitled 172
Olga Talalay
A departure is an arrival to someplace new 180
Veronika Opatřilová

6.Belonging _____
Simplicity and humility 190
Nausherwan Ghaffar
Perhaps because I have become a vegetarian 196
Angeliki Vlachou
A Mexican dreamer in corporate Sweden 214
Marco Guadarrama

About the editor 221

Introduction by the editor

Sofi Tegsveden Deveaux

A few years ago, a number of headlines in international media caught my attention. They were all reporting on the same subject matter: apparently, Sweden had introduced a six-hour work day. As most articles focused on the practical consequences and benefits of this, the scope of this measure was unclear, although it was easy to draw the conclusion that this was a nation-wide initiative improving the overall life quality for the majority of the population. However, from my desk in Stockholm, although admittedly being self-employed, I certainly wasn't enjoying a six hour working day. What I learnt at a much later stage, was that this hype had been generated by a very small trial conducted at a nursing home in the south west of Sweden.

The assumption that the whole working population of Sweden had reduced their work time by 25% is interesting, but not because it was untrue — or at least exaggerated. It is intriguing because it *could* have been true. Fitting so well with the image of Sweden as the Utopia of work-life balance, it was accepted without question. In general, most Swedish employers do prioritise the long-term well-being of the employees over the short-term profit of the company. Sweden is, in many ways, a very good place to work in, at least if you enjoy time off. Although the eight hour working day is predominately the norm, this number is not a guide, but a practice that most people adhere to, regardless of position and industry. It is perfectly acceptable and expected to leave at the end of your eight hour working day. Personal life is respected and prioritised over deadlines or staying later than the boss. The buffer provided by social security is not to be dismissed, crucially providing job protection and paid support for short or long term illness. Being a working parent is also an easy ride compared to many other countries, the generous 480 days of paid parental leave per child, paid days to stay at home to care for sick children and heavily subsidised child care all contribute to a very good work-life balance.

The reason I read these articles in the first place is my work. I am a Swedish language teacher and cultural trainer. This means that the people I meet on an everyday basis come from all over the world, with the intention of settling in Sweden for a shorter or longer periods of time. Some are still in the very early stages of planning their move, some just recently arrived.

Others have been here for months, years, and still others even consider themselves new in the country although they have lived and worked in Sweden for decades. I play an important role in their settling process, answering their questions, explaining, directing. I encourage, discourage, congratulate and console.

Our discussions are, naturally, based not only on their personal experiences, but also on the information and resources available through governmental agencies and the media. Such information is often bureaucratic in nature, sometimes with an ideological agenda or commercial motives. In certain instances, like the above mentioned articles, it is more sensational than factual. It rarely touches on the more complex reality that facing a new culture involves. Here, experiences shared by family, friends and new contacts sought out through online forums serve a purpose in providing real-life, unmediated accounts of the whats, wheres, hows and whys. These stories tend to be more personal, practically applicable and, although biased and anecdotal, easier to relate to in that they are tentative rather than affirmative.

One topic that always comes up is work. A job provides a necessary source of income and something to do with the days, but more importantly, it creates a sense of belonging and identity. The working environment gives a social framework which is a significant part of settling into a new place. Personally, I find discussions on work, culture and identity intriguing. It is these environments where the interface between each individual and others is pressingly imperative. Regardless of cultural origin or background, any career is dependent not only on ourselves and our capabilities, but also the social contract with our co-workers, superiors, and business contacts. While trying to achieve our own career goals and professional aspirations, others constantly contextualise us. We are forced to deal with other's opinions about us and their support or rejection of our goals. In that, I believe that the the context of work is an honest and sometimes brutal mirror of the dominant culture, its rules, its fallacies, its myths and its realities. By looking at the small-scale interactions of organisational culture, we can draw conclusions on society as a whole.

This is a topic that is relevant far beyond my own circles. In 2017, one out of six of the Swedish population was born outside the country. Although the proportion of this group in employment is lower, we are still dealing with a substantial number that cannot be ignored on a demographic, economic or societal level. This is a large, diverse and important group. Still, it is remarkably silent. News reporting and political discourse are increasingly angled towards the newly arrived, the outsiders, the anonymous masses, the numbers. The occasional individual experience is featured mostly as a representative of a larger narrative, setting an example, concretizing the intangible, proving a point.

What is lacking is the first-person perspective, told without a predetermined outcome. Hence, the idea for this project. Through this collection of real-life stories, my aim is to find a format for foreign-born professionals to share and reflect on their experiences, uninterfered and, although not necessarily unpolitical, depoliticized.

It is a vast topic, and a project that required courage and belief in my ability to assemble the incoherent into something coherent — without reiteration. This fittingly reflects the experience of starting a new life in a new place, as the final destination, or product, is unknown. There is no going back, no un-doing; there are promises to keep. Just like when moving to a new place, I had expectations, fears and hopes. Would the contributors interpret the topic the way I had in mind? Is the theme of work substantial and broad enough to give room for so many accounts?

In retrospect and with the final contributions in hand, the theme of work appears more as a pretext for something much more specific, at the same time universal, that the contributors have touched upon in their writing. Their stories tell not so much of the clinical ups and downs of a career journey, but rather the bewildering enterprise of being human, exposed to not only the surrounding environment and social context, but also our own personal shortcomings, values and aspirations, brought into light through a new cultural lens. From these stories, I am made to believe that when we are — as per our own will or circumstances — removed from our familiar environment, our identities are questioned and exposed in a new light. The boundaries between ourselves and what is around us are amplified, sore. With that, the specific location of Sweden has in effect been reduced, providing a framework only to delineate the human condition of dealing with oneself and others.

My selection of experiences or stories also stencils out the stories that are not being told. Of course, there was a number of submissions that we had to reject. Ironically, and sadly, the majority of the rejected contributions addressed the struggles of finding employment in Sweden, where the endings were rarely happy. My rejection of their chapters were just one in a line of many. This is in itself a paradox, probably being the most important story to tell.

I am also fully aware that beyond my own extended network of international professionals — including the contributors of this book — there is a much less privileged demographic group of foreign-born individuals not being represented here. I will not claim that the latter in any way deserve less respect or attention. However, feelings of loneliness, isolation and confusion — some of the many themes brought up in the following chapters — arguably apply to almost anyone that moves from one country to another, regardless of educational level or financial power.

By creating a channel for sharing these feelings, experiences and reflections, I am hoping also to challenge the expectations many people have when looking forward to a new life in Sweden. If you come to Sweden and expect Utopia to come to you, you will certainly be disappointed. But this doesn't mean that Sweden can't provide a good platform for a new life. From what I have learnt from my clients, friends and the contributors of this book, I am confident to claim that there are opportunities to build a good life here — but you will need to work for it. The six-hour working day is still not a reality, but six weeks' holiday — although not a legal entitlement — is a perfectly reasonable thing to ask for.

Stockholm, September 2018

Glossary

alien Belonging to a foreign country: 'An alien culture.'

asylum seeker A person who has left their home country as a political refugee and is seeking asylum in another: 'Only asylum seekers who are granted refugee status are allowed to work in the country.'

colonist A settler in or inhabitant of a colony: 'In the years following the Great War land was taken away from the inhabitants and given to colonists.'

emigrant A person who leaves their own country in order to settle permanently in another: 'She was a Polish emigrant who came to Scotland during the Second World War.'

émigré A person who has left their own country in order to settle in another, typically for political reasons: 'Soviet émigrés and defectors.'

expat Short for expatriate.

expatriate A person who lives outside their native country: 'American expatriates in London.'

foreigner A person born in or coming from a country other than one's own: 'This foreigner was born in Japan, as were his parents.'

immigrant A person who comes to live permanently in a foreign country: 'They found it difficult to expel illegal immigrants.'

incomer A person who has come to live in an area in which they have not grown up, especially in a close-knit rural community: 'An English incomer to Orkney.'

international talent [international] Existing, occurring, or carried on between nations: 'international trade' & [talent] People possessing natural aptitude or skill: 'I signed all the talent in Rome.'

migrant A person who moves from one place to another, especially in order to find work or better living conditions: 'We will not turn our back on these or other migrants contributing so much to our economy and our society.'

newcomer A person who has recently arrived in a place: 'She's a newcomer to the area.'

pioneer A person who is among the first to explore or settle a new country or area: 'They are explorers and pioneers in the great tradition like Columbus and Cook who sailed across the oceans.'

refugee A person who has been forced to leave their country in order to escape war, persecution, or natural disaster: 'Tens of thousands of refugees fled their homes.'

settler A person who moves with a group of others to live in a new country or area: 'The early European settlers in America were often fleeing from religious persecution.'

stranger A person who does not know, or is not known in, a particular place or community: 'I'm a stranger in these parts.'

The Oxford Dictionary of English

1. Why write?

Writing is sharing. It is a means for passing on our thoughts and experiences to others. There is a sense of solidarity in this, a belief in humanity and our own responsibility to disclose our mistakes and conclusions. Others will catch up where we have left.

Writing is also a mediating process. Through formulating and re-formulating our sentences, we filter and select — not only the words that best match our message, but also what fragments of reality we consider significant enough to tell. By staging our narrative, we can distance ourselves from the senseless, bringing meaning also to an inconsequential existence.

1

Flush
Kateřina Duchoňová

Not a Swedish class
Morag Ramsey

A recipe for a successful work life in Sweden
Adriana Salazar

Kateřina Duchoňová

Country of origin: Czech Republic.
Profession and occupation: I am currently working in a book shop and translating a crime novel from Swedish into Czech while finishing up my own novel.
Arrived in Sweden: 2012.
Reason for coming to Sweden: I wanted to live in Sweden because I had fallen in love with the country.
Reason for leaving Sweden: I fell ill and wanted to go through my medical treatment in my homeland.

Flush

The stage is in darkness. The audience has slowly stopped talking, making crunchy sounds and giggling. The show is about to begin. Two female voices break the silence and we enter the scene somewhere in the middle of the conversation.

'… because they are so blinded and they don't want to see. You know what I mean? They think it's enough to just fly to Thailand or New York and they have seen it all. Then they come back to Sweden, back to their comfortable lives, and think they know things.'

'But they're unwilling to realise it. They'd feel they'd have to change something and change is unpleasant, change hurts.'

'They're deep down in the fur.'

'What?'

'Like in *Sophie's world*, most people stay deep in the rabbit's fur.'

'Yes, that's exactly it.'

'But there are only a few who are curious enough and brave enough to want to see more. To want to climb to the top of the rabbit's hair to see things.'

'Like children and philosophers.'

'There are those who want to know the answers to the eternal questions of life.'

At that moment a reflector slowly illuminates the left part of the stage. There is an open shower cubicle. A young girl in her twenties, dressed in shorts and a vest top, is standing inside, spraying a bathroom cleaner all around and then scrubbing. Her hair is pinned up, she's barefoot. She's all red in the face; you can't tell if it's caused by the hard work or the heated conversation.

Another reflector throws light to the right corner of the stage. Another girl is bending over a toilet bowl. Her hair is short; a clip holds her fringe from falling into her eyes. She holds a toilet brush in her right hand, trying to keep her face as far from it as possible. She's dressed like the other girl. A t-shirt and a pair of shorts. She's all sweaty. She flushes the toilet and sits down on the floor.

'I don't think anyone uses this bathroom anyway. The one downstairs is always way worse.'

'You're right. I think so too.'

'But I like Anders' house. Because he's a nice guy and he's always satisfied. I like those customers.'

'I prefer those who aren't at home.'

'Of course! Me too! But we can forget about those, you know why? Because we, unlike the rest of the girls, speak Swedish.'

'You think?'

'Sure! Evelina from Poland doesn't speak a word! She only speaks English and that's why she gets customers who aren't at home.'

'I hate that. Shouldn't it be a good thing that we speak the language?'

'Not in our world. Evelina wouldn't mind talking to the customers if she could. We have a problem with that because we're fucking socio-phobic weirdos.'

'Yeah, I know. But there are some things everybody must have a problem with, aren't there? Like yesterday when 'sleeping beauty' was snoring on the couch in the living room while we were trying to tidy up in there. I mean they only have cleaning service come over once every two weeks; how hard is it not to forget to fall asleep?'

'Or remember to wake up — like that girl of our age who was still in bed with her one-night-stand while her dad was urging us to clean her room, too.'

'Or not to leave sex toys on the bedside table.'

'Yuck, what?!'

'Haven't I told you? That must have been when I was with Evelina doing the spring-clean. There was this granddad. But not like Anders, he was really a terrible sort. He was the kind who likes to act younger. But he was eighty! I know that because he had a congratulations card on the shelf. When we came he was wearing a bathrobe! And you know how I hate to see people's feet. I saw legs too, wrinkled, disgusting, naked legs. I will never recover.'

'And the toys?'

'Oh yeah… that's the only thing you want to know, you pervert! So I went to the bedroom and started dusting and

suddenly saw a dildo on the wifey's little table. What the fuck!'
'Remind me why we're doing this?'

'I don't know.'

'You see I don't even know how people can hire a cleaning person. Because the things that we see... home is such a personal thing! I could never imagine a stranger coming to my flat and going through every little thing like we do in their houses!'

'That reminds me of something. You know I go to those Swedish as a second language lessons? Last time our teacher came and she was all shaky and stressed. You could tell she had been crying. Then she explained that somebody had broken into her flat and she said the worst thing wasn't the things they had taken, but the fact some stranger had been there, invading her personal space.'

'I bet she also has a cleaning girl.'

'Maybe she does.'

'The thing is she knows the girl. She has seen her face and concluded that she doesn't mind that this person from an eastern country comes to her house and cleans her mess.'

'Because to them you're not even a person, don't you understand?'

'I think we take it too seriously. To us a home is a sacred place. But it doesn't have to be that way for everybody.'

'Because people lack imagination.'

'Maybe. Yes, you're right. For example, about us. What the hell do they know about us? Nothing. They think we're idiots, some good-for-nothings from a country they mistake for Chechnya. And it offends me, I hate that idea. I can see it in their shallow smiles.'

'Imagine. You, coming from a post-communist country, from a family who hates the old regime more than anything. A couple of months doing the cleaning work and you suddenly turn into a confirmed socialist.'

'Noo, no. That's not it. I hate this kind of job. I hate being looked down upon by somebody who cannot learn another language or remember the names of countries. Or by some mother who welcomes you with a frozen smile and you see that she is offended that her cleaning lady is not some ugly monster but someone who looks good and who probably also has a life. But like I say, it's me. I don't like that. But take Evelina. She doesn't seem to mind.'

'No, Evelina enjoys cleaning. She always tells me that she keeps telling our boss she wants more work. When she comes home she has nothing to do.'

'But she didn't come to Sweden to live her life, to explore or go to rock concerts, like us. She came to make money. And guess what. With her husband they're saving up for a house like this one or one of those she cleans every day. Only they want to build it back in Poland.'

'They're happy then.'

'They are.'

'But we have to quit.'

'Or we'll go crazy.'

'And we'll take our revenge.'

'How?'

'We'll write a novel, a detective story. It will be one of those Scandinavian thrillers. And our most hated customers will be there. The giant man who always pats my shoulder as if I was a little girl.'

'The fake-smile freak who cleans her house before we come

and urges us to find the two bacteria she has left there for us to find otherwise she makes complaints.'

'The Finnish *mamma* who is always at home with only one child and doesn't manage to clean her house, which is actually pretty small.'

'The guy in the offices who always does number two right before I have to go and clean that bathroom.'

'But what will the plot be?'

'I don't know. Somebody kills the cleaning girl and the murderer will be one of them.'

'I don't like that, thank you very much.'

'Then we can write about us. I see it as a play. One of those shows where there are only two actors on the stage, nothing much is happening, the dialogue is what matters the most.'

'I'm loving this. Two cleaning ladies discussing deep stuff.'

'It could start with a moment of surprise. You won't know at first what they're doing.'

'The stage will be in darkness.'

Morag Ramsey

Country of origin: Canada.
Profession: Historian.
Current occupation: Doctoral student.
Arrived in Sweden: 2013.
Reason for coming to Sweden: I met a charming Swedish man.
Reason for staying in Sweden: I am happy here!
Other: I am a doctoral student at the department of history of science and ideas at Uppsala University. I work within a project centring around foetal research in Sweden, and many of the words I draw are words I picked up from work.

Not a Swedish class
Introduction by the editor

Morag Ramsey's sketches are the result of an on-going record of her Swedish language learning. This seemingly arbitrary selection of words, taken out of their context, tells of the non-linear process of vocabulary acquisition as well as the vulnerable and sometimes even absurd experience of being in a learner's position. This lexicon also forms a narrative on its own, reflecting the reality from where it has been collected, giving us a glimpse into what concepts and situations Ramsey herself encounters — and deems significant.

Knapp

- word meaning barely

- common everyday use: yes

- pronounced: Knupp

Knepig

- word meaning tricky

- common everyday use: yes

- pronounced: Kne–pig
  ↳ like there

You know, chess has always been Knepigt for me. And I don't want to play that card, but it might be because I'm a dog.

Are you serious? I'm a mouse...

Lyhörd

- word meaning sensitive

- common everyday use: not very

- pronounced: lea-herd

En nackdel

- word meaning disadvantage, drawback

- Common everyday use: YEP

- pronounced: nuck-del
  └─ there

what are the nackdelar of hiring a full-time tummy rubber? Glad you asked. As you can see, there are none.

2018

DOG TUMMY RUBS

Rimlig

- word meaning reasonable, fair plausible

- common everyday use: Yeah

- pronounced: rim-lig

I think that it is rimligt that you don't move while I nap.

Undanröja

- word meaning remove
  (an obstacle)

- common everyday use: nah

- pronounced: oond-un-ruy-ah

Finally I've undanröjt a major obstacle to my daily happiness.

DOG FOOD

Ödmjukast

- word meaning humbly

- common everyday use: No

- pronounced: ud - myuk- ust

> Dear Person,
> You are hereby invited to
> my buffet lunch, which
> you will also provide.
> ödmjukast,
> Dog.

Adriana Salazar

Country of origin: Venezuela.
Profession: International relations.
Current occupation: Accounting consultant.
Arrived in Sweden: 2010.
Reason for coming to Sweden: A rapidly deteriorating socio-economic and security situation in Venezuela, responsible for the largest exodus of population in the country's history.
Reason for staying in Sweden: I have nothing left in my home country, and the situation in the country has become worse. Also, I have my own family in Sweden now.

A recipe for a successful work life in Sweden (that I wish I could have had)

Ingredients:

- One computer*
- Some money for application fees and some more for networking
- Internet access*
- Tons of patience
- One means of transportation of choice
- Basic computer skills
- One office suite (like Microsoft Office or free alternatives such as Open Office or Google Docs)*
- One Swedish-speaking friend
- A myriad of social skills
- One fistful of positivity
- One bucket of charm

- One bundle of endurance
- One chunk of flexibility
- Faith and hope to season
- One gram of serendipity.

* Can be used for free at any public library in Sweden.

Instructions:

1.

Enrol in a Swedish course and make an effort to learn the language. Yes, perhaps you're looking to work in an international setting with English as the working language. Yes, Swedes are exceptionally good at English. However, being able to speak some Swedish will open a lot of doors and will help you melt the (rather thick) social ice. If you're waiting for the Migration Board to make a decision about your migratory status and thus cannot enrol in *SFI* (Swedish for Immigrants, the government-sponsored language course), do enrol in a private course if you have the means. Otherwise, get creative! You can, for example, borrow language books for free from the public library and visit coffee shops known as *språkkaféer* (language coffee shops) that organise evenings where people wanting to learn a certain language can meet and talk.

2.

If you have a high school diploma, a vocational education diploma and/or a university degree from abroad, open your computer, connect to the internet and visit the web site www.uhr.se. Click on 'Recognition of foreign qualifications' and follow the steps to apply to have your foreign studies evaluated. You will require some patience to wait until a decision is made, but UHR's validation can be very valuable for the future. It could tell potential employers what your diploma from abroad is equivalent to in Sweden, or allow you to apply for higher studies.

3.

Take your means of transportation of choice and go straight to your local Swedish Public Employment Service (*Arbetsförmedlingen*) in order to register as an employment seeker. Ask them if your profession is regulated (some of these include lawyers, doctors, nurses, dentists and teachers) and, if that's the case, ask them to refer you to the governmental authority that regulates your profession. You will have to complete extra steps in this case, so get in touch with the relevant authority as soon as possible and gather information about the requirements that you will have to meet in order to be able to practise your profession in Sweden.

You should also ask your case worker at the Swedish Public Employment Service if you benefit from any labour market programmes. You can, for example, gain access to free career coaching (although do ask how that will or might affect your income), or potential employers could qualify for state subsidies if they employ you (although be mindful that this might attract the wrong kind of employers; try to figure out if their intention is to eventually hire you or to just take advantage of cheap labour).

4.

Go back to your computer and open your internet browser of choice to find out which trade union exists for your profession. There are trade unions for most professions, or at least for big professional groups: trade unions for engineers, trade unions for economists, trade unions for academics, etc. Visit their web site and apply to become a member of both their trade union and their unemployment insurance fund (*a-kassa*). Most people are put off by the high membership fees, but not everyone knows that trade unions offer lower fees for students and the unemployed. Trade unions are rather unknown to most foreigners, and are even underestimated by many Swedes, but this step is crucial. In order to be eligible to receive somewhat decent unemployment benefits, you need to have been a member of a trade union and an unemployment insurance fund for between one and one and a half years. Otherwise it might be difficult to survive on the basic unemployment benefits provided by *Alfa-kassan*, the governmental entity that administers the general basic insurance. Moreover, trade unions are an invaluable source of support should you have any problems with an employer. They can, for example, help you collect unpaid wages, offer you free legal advice, help with your CV and covering letter, provide interview training, seminars, magazines and even some career coaching.

5.

Keep working on your computer, but this time take your basic computer skills and open your office suite of choice to create a standard CV and a covering letter. There are plenty of tips on how to write the perfect application. In my opinion, the first thing you should remember is to keep it simple – think Scandinavian minimalism. For your CV, state your work experience and education and provide very brief explanations about your achievements in each one. Do not repeat your CV for your covering letter, write instead about what your professional goals are and why they should hire you (of all applicants). It is very important to ask your Swedish-speaking friend to help you translate it into proper Swedish. Don't forget your trade union! They can provide valuable feedback. Truth be told, neither your CV nor your covering letter will matter much to your professional success, but they're a formality that you need to complete.

6.

Use your standard CV and covering letter to create a LinkedIn profile as well as profiles in the biggest recruitment agencies. Racism in the work market is a real issue in Sweden, but recruitment agencies make money from finding the most qualified people and are thus less prone to discrimination — keep an eye on them!

7.

Subscribe to as many job alerts as possible: LinkedIn, recruitment agencies where you've created profiles, *Arbetsförmedlingen*. Edit your settings to receive alerts daily — or as frequently as possible. Some positions are filled before the application deadline has passed, so always apply as soon as possible.

8.

Take all of your social skills and network 'til you drop. Spice it up with lots of positivity and charm. This is another crucial step: the reality is that most jobs in Sweden are obtained through contacts or recommendations, not necessarily your merits. Make sure you meet a lot of different people; introduce yourself and let them know that you're looking for a job.

Meeting people in Sweden can be challenging, but there are plenty of fora that will serve your purposes. Almost every city is represented in a LinkedIn group that organises weekly lunches — connect online and in real life. Specialised networking organisations such as the Rotary club and Internations are worth looking up. Another great way to meet people is by engaging in a hobby or sport: a dance course, a painting class — take the opportunity to build bridges with people. Or why not the *språkkafé*, where you can kill two birds with one stone by meeting people while improving your Swedish at the same time.

9.

Keep a close eye on those job alerts and apply, apply, apply! Mix a handful of patience with a lot of endurance so that you don't get discouraged by all of the negative answers that you'll most likely get at the beginning. Open your computer and your office suite and apply some more basic computer skills to adapt your standard CV and covering letter to each and every single job application (even if they might be a formality). Your trade union can provide you with guidance on how to do this and, if you're called for an interview, they can even help you prepare with a mock interview.

10.

Take out your flexibility and be prepared to apply for less qualified jobs. Also be prepared to apply for internships (often unpaid, although you might receive some compensation from the Public Employment Service if they approve the placement). Unless you have a profession that is in demand (such as IT genius, engineering or life sciences), you should be prepared to take some steps back — hopefully to make a leap forward later on.

11.

Do not only apply to advertised jobs. Send an open application to companies where you think you'd like to work. Be consistent and follow up. Call them and ask them about the status of your application and, if you're rejected, ask the recruiter for feedback on your application.

12.

This is the moment to bring in faith and hope. The wheels are in motion and the road might be long and bumpy, but your efforts will eventually crystallize into an offer. One gram of serendipity and it could just happen overnight. When you do get an offer, get in touch again with your trade union for advice on salaries and working conditions. They can even go through your contract to make sure that everything is in order. It is also a good idea to inform yourself about your duties and rights as an employee; unfortunately it's not rare to hear stories about not-so-serious employers taking advantage of migrants in vulnerable positions.

Optional

If you have the possibility (or if it is taking a long time to find a job), take the opportunity to reflect upon your career. What do you really want to do with it? Analyse the status of your local work market: where do you fit in? Are there any gaps that you can fill, any needs that you can cover? Is there a lot of competition or is your profession in demand? If not, could it be the right time to make a career change? Get a mentor! Organisations like Rotary often have projects to mentor newcomers.

There are many things about working life in Sweden that will make you frustrated but, at the same time, the country offers endless opportunities to develop. The education system caters for a wide range of needs, from individual courses in specific subjects to vocational studies and university degrees; education is accessible and often free. You can apply for subsidies during your study and finance the rest of your costs with a low-interest rate student loan that you can repay once you are employed.

Or perhaps you have always dreamt of having your own company? Small enterprises are the backbone of the Swedish economy and, therefore, the state has developed a series of initiatives to encourage entrepreneurship: free mentorship programmes, financing, subsidies, seminars. You can build the career that you want for yourself, provided that you know what you want, how to get it and that you work hard for it.

2. Leap

Between leaving and arriving there is a gap, a prolonged moment of uncertainty. The unpredictable nature of this interim gives a sense of freedom, adventure, and that fate is in our hands. Anything and everything may happen, and the lack of predictability inspires courage.

Taking the decision to leave for another place, regardless of reason and motives, requires determination, but also faith in that everything will work out according to our plans. However, as reality kicks in, plans are re-written, hope is reconciled and we have to admit our dependency on others. Left in a new territory where we lack the means for navigation, we are back to being children, helpless and forced to rely on trust.

Pride may sometimes stand in the way of taking the right decision, but we should remember that disappointment is always coupled with relief.

You are the hero of this story
Catherine Derieux

Home
Clarissa Hirst

Some reverse American dreams
Joshua Bookman

Photo Credit: Lætitia Derieux/Native Image Station

Catherine Derieux

Country of origin: France.
Profession: Writer.
Arrived in Sweden: 2016.
Reason for coming to Sweden: I fell in love with the country.
Reason for staying in Sweden: I am still in love with the country.
Other: Author of *Portraits de Stockholm*, a French city guide introducing travellers to the Swedish capital through the eyes of its inhabitants.

You are the hero of this story

You want to learn a new language. You love idioms and the texture of foreign words in your mouth. How crisp they are under your teeth when you don't know yet how to pronounce them properly, and then how they melt on your tongue once you get used to them. But you're indecisive. Should you get a bite of spicy Japanese or a taste of *doce* Portuguese? Wait, there's something more on the menu. A rather unpretentious dish, seemingly simple, but with its very own zest — Swedish. So Japanese, Portuguese or Swedish? Which one would be the most delicious?

If you chose Japanese, keep reading **A**. *If you'd rather go with Portuguese, see you in* **B**. *If you prefer Swedish, go to* **C**.

A

You try Japanese. It's a challenge. The syntax is as weird as a *daifuku's* texture. Chewy, unexpected. You never know how to sprinkle your sentences with particles, so you throw はs, がs, にs, のs and もs around as if they were burning your tongue. And don't get started on the writing systems. Yes, systemzZz, as in *plural*. 'What have I got myself into?' you ask, and then wonder, 'how do I say that in Japanese?' Maybe you're more hooked that you thought. Surprised by this revelation, you hang in there — lost in translation — in a world where *hi* suddenly means yes, and where *sayonara* (the one word you actually felt confident uttering) is actually to avoid at all costs. You're puzzled and your mind is in pieces. Even with all your efforts, Japanese remains an impregnable fort.

Discouraged, you need a fresh start. You decide to switch to Portuguese. Go to **B**. *You can't help it: you still love the language. You decide to switch gears. Go to* **D**

B

You try Portuguese, love it, move to Rio. You get drunk during the carnival and dance your head off. You meet a guy — he's handsome and funny and smart. He likes your weird French accent and your thirst for adventure. You're in love. But he's only in Brazil on holiday. He has to get back to his country, to his life. You decide to pack up your own life once again and follow him. You smash your piggy bank and scrape under the couch pillows hoping to find a few extra cents. And you get yourself a shiny ticket to the other side of the ocean. The day before your flight, that cute guy finally decides to tell you he isn't only going back to his country and his life, but also to his girlfriend. You're gutted, but it's too late to back-pedal anyway, right? Right.

Go to **E**.

C _____

You try Swedish. It's not too hard, but the language's melody seems off. Or it's just your ear that's not tuned right. The vowels sound high-pitched and bang into the deep consonants. You may not be a Carl Bellman of Germanic languages, but you kind of like Swedish anyway. Especially those ornate As and Os. And yet, you stumble and fall out of practice. A few months pass and you finally get back on your grammar's back. You know everything about *fika* and *lagom*, but apart from ordering coffee with a piece of cake, or your steak medium rare, you feel stuck. You're lacking direction.

So you take off and go north north north — here's a direction for you! You book yourself a nice vacation. ABBA, IKEA, *kanelbullar, svenska* — you mutter to yourself in the cobblestoned streets of sweet *Gamla Stan*. You get drunk on New Year's Eve and dance your head off. You see the fireworks spangle along Stockholm's skyline — it's dazzling and thrilling and galvanizing. You're in love. But you're only here on holiday. How could you go back to your bland life in your country? Everything here seems more colourful, more flavourful. You're not even on the plane taking you back home yet and you're already plotting how to put down roots in Viking territory.

You're quite impulsive; you don't give yourself time to catch your breath and book a ticket on a whim. You're unprepared and you don't care! Go to **E**. *You're meticulous; you carefully lay the groundwork with your eyes on the prize. Go to* **D**.

D_____

You've signed up for a course. You're unexpectedly nervous, but you're determined. You want to make progress in the language, you're going to make progress. You'd listen to *Eye of the Tiger* in a loop if it weren't distracting you from your vocabulary lists. First day. You've got your books, your notepad, your pen, your dictionary, but it seems like you forgot your voice. The first few lessons, you're as mute as a newt. But at least the newt knows how to use her tongue. To avoid being in the teacher's gaze, you look down, write down everything. Your neck hurts from holding your always-bent head. You go one word at a time. One awkwardly constructed sentence at a time. One textbook page at a time. You watch unintelligible TV shows, parroting dialogues that are just a mash of sounds to your mashing ears. No matter how hard you try, your mouth never gets in shape and sings flat. Some people are flat-footed, you're just flat-mouthed. So be it. Your mental soundtrack just switches from *Survivor* to Rihanna and you work, work, work and work. Before you know it, it's your last class.

You're studying Japanese: After working so hard, you still feel unable to have a real conversation in the language. You realise you may have bitten off more than you could chew. You decide to go for something a little bit easier. Go back to **C**. *You're studying Japanese: After working so hard, you deserve a treat. You smash your piggy bank and scrape under the couch pillows to find a few extra cents. If you're learning a language, you should get the chance to speak it in the country, right? Right. Go to* **F**. *You're studying Swedish: you've come a long way and made progress. Now it's time for the fun part! Go to* **I**.

E _____
Welcome to Sweden!

You're freezing cold, you have a runny nose and one orphan glove. You're a mess, but you're weirdly happy. *Mamma Mia*, here you are! You crash in an outrageously overly priced Airbnb while refreshing *Blocket's* web page every 30 seconds. But nobody wants to rent a flat to you because you don't have a job. Or Swedish references. How come freelancing for clients in a foreign country doesn't count? You're a writer, or you used to be… Now you have to dig deep into your childhood memory and do some introspection to find out what else you could be good at (you, who would copycat Beckett's *bon qu'à ça*), to come up with a new career plan on the go. If this were a movie, this would be the moment for a fade out, and a shot showing [insert relevant childhood memories nobody cares about]. But this is not a movie. So you just send out résumés for job ads you're remotely interested in, and remotely qualified for. But weeks later, still nothing. You're confused.

You get bored and decide to go home. Go to **H***. You decide to explore new horizons. You keep applying for English-speaking administrative jobs, but also take a shot at positions in the travel industry where your language skills might be an asset. Go to* **L***. You decide to change your strategy and get serious this time. You sign up for* Lunchback, *a clever networking app, to get Swedish people to give you feedback on your résumé and covering letter, and start volunteering a few hours a week in order to get a Swedish reference. Go to* **N***.*

F _____

Konnichiwa Japan! You land in Tokyo and your head spins. You float to your flat share in a trance. The first night, you wander around Shinjuku. The neon lights buzz, bumping sounds come out the *pachinko* centres along with a breeze of AC. High-school girls in uniforms and ponytails walk alongside drunk salarymen in suits and male hosts with sculptured haircuts. The next day you jump into the Odeo line toward Kuramae. The July sun dries the air and scorches your skin. You don't care. You walk along the Sumida river, its dark waters undulate like a giant snake. Soon, you reach Asakusa and a wide intersection stripped with crosswalks. Here, Kaminarimon, the Thunder gate, rises in the sun. The crowd rushes and hustles under its imposing red lantern, flooding Nakamise-dori, this shambles of a street lined with colourful shops. Everywhere you look, it's a profusion of kitschy magnets, key rings and figurines, flashy masks, and snacks and sweets wrapped in sparkling paper. The backstreets are much quieter. You greet old ladies wrapped up in elegant *yukata* and perched on *geta*. They sit in front of traditional wooden houses, their wrinkled faces all smiles for you. One day in Tokyo and you're under its spell. You wish your treat could become a permanent feast.

But reality soon catches up. You can barely have a conversation with the locals. English is rarely an option. You're illiterate in this country. How could you get a job here, let alone a career? That can't stop you. But a big scare of an earthquake followed by a nuclear crisis might. You love Japan deeply, but you're not sure you see yourself living there anymore. Your family's insistence on your coming back to safer territory makes you give in. The plane takes off, the runway gets smaller and smaller as you rush towards the sky. You have tears in your eyes.

You quit learning languages. You quit traveling. Japan was your true love, nothing will be as good. Let's go home. Let's go to **H**. *Back home, you experience a reverse culture shock. Your brain gets bored of listening only to your mother tongue all day. You need a change, something new to exhaust your hyperactive neurons. Welcome to* **C**. *Back home, you can't shake off* *this sadness that sank into your body after leaving Japan. To cheer you up, your mum takes you on a trip. Let's go somewhere you know nothing about for a few days! Now boarding in* **G**.

G _____

You spend a few days in Göteborg, roaming the cobbled streets of Haga, getting high on the local Lipstick, this white and red building overlooking the city, getting acquainted with the local tradition of *fika*. Then you spend a few hours in a train, your face glued to the window. Lakes follow forests follow lakes. Finally Stockholm. The city kisses the water at every corner, stunned by the beauty of its own reflection. Stony heads framed by gold, crowns sitting on the ridges of a bridge, runic tales engraved in old walls.

The visit doesn't come short of surprises. Nothing could feel further away from Japan than Sweden. And yet, you can't shake that feeling of familiarity and belonging. There's something in the summer air that reminds you of your lost foreign home. A quietness. A peacefulness. A politeness. Maybe it's the way people walk, unrushed. At two extremes on the hierarchy ladder, you surprisingly find the same respect for each other. Maybe it's the elegance, this taste for aesthetics that touches everything. Sure, the Nordic style doesn't really compare with *tatami, fusuma* and lacquer. Still, there is a common minimalism, clean lines, natural materials. Or maybe it's the rituals? *Fika* versus tea ceremony? You really couldn't say. But just like that, you're in love again. The getaway is coming to an end. There's only one solution. You'll learn Swedish and come back!

You're quite impulsive: you don't give yourself time to catch your breath and book a ticket on a whim. You're unprepared and you don't care! Go to **E**. *You're meticulous: you carefully lay the groundwork with your eyes on the prize. Go to* **I**.

H _____
What? You're giving up? No way! Get back and try again!

I _____
Welcome to Sweden!

Long time no see, but this little reunion makes you happy. You land at Arlanda, and you know where to go. You've networked until exhaustion — from your (ex) co-worker's neighbour's son who's doing an Erasmus at KTH University to your cousin's boyfriend's cousin who fell in love with a Swede, a typical love refugee. Thanks to your connections, you've found a room in a reasonably overpriced flat share in Södermalm. A near miracle.

Now, all you need is a job. With your shaky Swedish, you knew in advance it wouldn't be easy — especially for a copywriter. But you're ready to take a career turn. You've considered your options before moving, of course. You're well organised and meticulous, you're not afraid of paperwork and you have an eye for detail, you got this, girl! That basic administrative course you took last month will pay off, you're sure of it. You dissect *Arbetsförmedlingen*'s web site, you attend all those meet-ups for expats, you craft a beautiful résumé while hopping from *språkfika* to *språkfika* to keep refining your '*sju*' pronunciation. But weeks later, still nothing. You're confused.

You join a group of other job-hunting, non-Swedish women to share experiences and tips, and get a second opinion on your applications. Go to **J**. *You sign up for an intensive Swedish course to step up your game. With this new line on your résumé and some new-found confidence, you start applying for jobs in Swedish. Go to* **K**. *You decide to explore new horizons. You keep applying for English-speaking administrative jobs, but also take a shot at positions in the travel industry where your language skills might be an asset. Go to* **L**. *You do all of the above. Go to* **N**.

J ——————————————————————————

You start meeting once a week with this group of pretty cool ladies. They're literally from everywhere. You learn tons and get pretty insightful feedback. You feel energised, and you even make friends in the process! One of your job-hunting comrades is impressed by your attitude and your will to improve. Well done! She tips you off about an opening in her husband's company.

K _____

You have your first interview in Swedish. Your hands are sweaty and shaky, but you're also excited about this personal victory. Your wobbly language skills managed to convince someone, you hardly believe it. During the interview though, you realise your Swedish is not quite as good as you thought it was. It's one thing to write – you have time to look up words, check a grammar rule, or even ask a native speaker to correct your mistakes — but it's something else to have a professional conversation, let alone a proper job interview.

This stressful experience makes you realise you're not ready to take a job in Swedish. You go back to your classes and will return to your ansökningar *in a little while. In the meantime, you keep looking for English-speaking jobs. Go to* **N**. *You understand one sentence out of three of what the recruiter says, but you nod emphatically like you have it all under control. Luckily, you're good at catching clues and manage to answer all the questions thrown at you. You get out of the interview feeling like the David Copperfield of languages! Go to* **I**.

L _____

You have a job offer! A miraculous job offer in the tourism industry. Finally! But a few things are bugging you. The information you got about the position during the interview don't really match the job description. Also, the salary is extremely low (you've checked the *lönestatistik*, of course) and there's no room for negotiation. You're quite surprised. You had this rosy image about jobs in Sweden. You had heard so much about those cool start-ups that were going to change the world, and those world-renowned companies with their fancy salaries and their comfy benefits, you know, the Electroluxes and the Ericssons, the H&Ms and the IKEAs. Maybe you were wearing rose-tinted glasses. Maybe Sweden is not as shiny and perfect as you thought?

Anyway, you're too excited to get an offer at all; you jump at the chance and take the job. Go to **M**. *You politely ask for a few days to think about it. Once you've cooled off a little you decide to decline the offer. You know it's quite a risk to take, it's been tough to get there, but you hope a better opportunity will come your way. Go to* **N**.

M _____

The job turns out to be a living hell, sucking all joy out of you. You can't believe you went through all this trouble to end up so miserable.

You quit: you quit the job, you quit Sweden. Go to **H**. *You try to suck it up for a while, but it's soul-crushing. You decide to get back on the job hunt. Go to* **N**.

N _____

All your hard work finally paid off! You got an interview for a very exciting job that checks all your boxes. The ad mentioned both English and Swedish as mandatory. But since this is an international company, your foreign-tinted English and your imperfect Swedish turned out to be good enough. You're glad that you decided to apply even though you felt a little under-qualified language-wise. You're even gladder when the employer calls you back for a second interview. And you're over the moon when you actually get a mouth-watering offer for this sparkly cool trendy job. No second-guessing: you take it!

If this were a movie, this would be the happy end. But this is not a movie. And this isn't the ending. Fast forward to **O**.

O _____

Two years have passed. You're now pretty settled in your Swedish life. You're still working for that international company at that shiny job that you love. Soon after you started you got your *personnummer*, the modern Viking version of open sesame. You're still not completely idiomatic in the local language (will you ever be?), but you've dramatically improved. Everything's comfy now. So what should you do?

Should you ask for more responsibilities at your work to keep yourself challenged?

Should you pursue that childhood dream and try to break into the charity sector?

Should you reinvent yourself (again) and move to a new country?

Should you 'just' enjoy the beautiful life you've built for yourself with sweat and tears and bask in this outrageous comfort?

The possibilities are endless. The choice is yours. You're the hero of your own career after all. Of your own life. So… where to next?

Clarissa Hirst

Country of origin: Australia.
Profession: Digital content producer.
Current occupation: Working for a content marketing agency while travel writing and blogging on the side.
Arrived in Sweden: 2012.
Reason for coming to Sweden: As part of a gap year to learn the Swedish language and culture.
Reason for staying in Sweden: I met someone.
Reason for leaving Sweden: I was unhappy in my job, my relationship did not work out and I wanted to move back closer to family and friends.
Other: I am fascinated by language and landscapes, and my two greatest passions are writing and travelling.

Home

It's Christmas Eve 2017. I'm standing atop a yawning volcanic cone, staring down into the grassy crater as a group of Chinese tourists snap pictures excitedly behind me. If I look up and scan the surroundings, I can see numerous green lumps and bumps emerging from the otherwise flat landscape, an indication of the turbulent eruptions that brought about the existence of this place.

Directly ahead of me is the city skyline, dominated as always by the needle-like Sky Tower. Behind the skyscrapers lie the islands of the Hauraki Gulf, sitting calmly amidst crystal-blue water populated by a myriad of white triangles — sailing boats that are breezing past. And, of course, the ever-present Rangitoto, the 200-year-old volcano, looms in the foreground.

Up here on Mount Eden, gazing around at the surrounding city of Auckland, I feel happy, at ease and, perhaps above all else, at home. The warm sun and the cool breeze around my bare legs is familiar and appreciated. How different it is to the first Christmas I spent all the way on the other side of the world, in a countryside town called Kil in the Värmland region of Sweden.

I vividly recall sitting down to the veritable feast of the *julbord* for my very first Swedish Christmas. I remember the energetic *snaps* drinking songs, candles in the windows and the excitement of the children when *tomten* showed up at the front door. It was a beautiful time filled with new traditions, food and a cosy atmosphere so different to the sunshine-filled Yuletide celebrations I grew up with both in my home country of Australia and my father's birthplace, New Zealand.

/ /

I moved to Sweden in 2012 having decided to take a gap year to work as an au pair and learn a new language. Little did I know when I touched down just after my 22nd birthday that this northern place was to become my home away from home for three and a half years.

During that time, I went from being a monolingual Australian to a fluent Swedish speaker. I would spend a year struggling to chauffeur, cook for, dress, put to bed and do laundry for five Swedish children under the age of 12. I would start my own business, enter into a serious long-term relationship and begin what I believed would be a lifelong career in academia. I would acquire permanent Swedish residency and become engaged to a person I thought I would spend the rest of my life with.

And yet, despite all these life-changing episodes, in late 2016 I would book a one-way flight to New Zealand, and I have not set foot in Sweden since.

//

I have always possessed a strong determination. Sometimes, this manifests itself as positive ambition to strive towards achieving goals I set for myself. At other times, it turns into bouts of stubbornness in which I refuse to lose sight of what I've set my mind to, even when all signs point to the fact that I should let it go. Life in Sweden, for me, began as a challenge — to spend a year working abroad in a country learning about a culture totally different to my own, and to learn a foreign language, something I hadn't been able to do sitting in a classroom.

Little did I know just how challenging my new life would turn out to be. When people find out that I can speak Swedish, or that I spent a year taking care of five kids, they assume that these things must have been intensely difficult. They were. But being new to Sweden, I took everything in my stride as a learning experience. Everything was new and exciting, and every challenge I faced, while tough, I saw as character building. The real challenge of life in Sweden came later, after I began to settle there. After the initial excitement of living in a new country wore off. After the international friends I had made departed for their home countries when their six month exchange stints were over. After the novelty of a cold, dark winter turned into a harsh reality.

//

Sweden as a country is marvellous in so many ways. Everything is so efficient and modern, cycling is considered cool, attitudes towards gender equality, innovation and the benefits of spending time outdoors are all commendable and contribute to a quality of life other countries envy. But I experienced an intense loneliness in Sweden of the kind I'd never encountered before — a kind that left me feeling isolated, disconnected and totally unlike myself.

The reasons for this were many and complex, but one that I can pinpoint with certainty was my work situation. In a place where I didn't have any family or friends of my own, work would become the driver that kept me going. And when it didn't work out as I'd hoped, I became disheartened and dejected.

I spent a year or so in Sweden without work, at least in the conventional sense. After a year au pairing in Sweden, I'd returned for a brief period to Australia to finish my master's degree, before returning to Sweden again on a *sambo* visa, with the intention of finding a full-time job. And, just like many expats before me, the process would be more difficult than I had anticipated. I failed to find anything in my field and spent months unemployed. Due to this situation, combined with an absence of friends or family to speak of, and weather that made it difficult to be outside, I rapidly became unhappy.

Things picked up when I decided to start my own business. Realising that the job market was going to be difficult to crack, I decided to take things into my own hands and use my native language as a means of finding work. I set up a company offering proofreading and editing services for Swedish businesses publishing English content. I met a translator and, through her connections, started to pick up freelance editing jobs here and there. I made a small amount that was by no means enough to get by, but was enough to at least pay my share of the rent each month so I wasn't totally reliant on my partner for everything.

Eventually, I landed a PhD position at Karlstad University. This was a source of constant confusion to my friends back home, as in Australia a PhD position is considered study. In Sweden you're paid a salary. It's not an amazing salary, but it's definitely enough to live off. Academia at the time was my dream job, and to get paid to perform my own research, teach and learn every day seemed incredible to me. I supplemented this day job by picking up some more freelance work and also began doing some freelance travel writing and content marketing. For me, freelancing was initially a natural response to the difficulties of finding full-time work. But I kept it up, even after starting full-time work, as it gave me a purpose. My partner worked at the same university as me, we lived together and my entire social circle consisted of his friends and colleagues. We even worked out together at the gym and spent most of our free time together. Writing was the sole thing in my life that was my own, and I treasured it.

And so, I got into a routine where I got up at 5.30 a.m. each morning to work on my writing before heading to work from 8 a.m. until 4 p.m. Being the ambitious and determined person that I am, I was pleased with everything I was doing. I was going to get my PhD, I was doing what I loved on the side, and earning enough to get by. Slowly, the loneliness and disconnection began to dissipate. Through my freelancing, and from being active on social media, I forged connections with other expats in Sweden and travel bloggers both in Scandinavia and elsewhere. I joined an online group of creatives that I interacted with on a daily basis, getting inspiration for my various writing projects. These people, though I rarely met them in real life, gave me a little community outside of my life in Sweden that helped me feel like I wasn't so alone.

Travel also helped me to cope with the loneliness of being in Sweden, and I even incorporated it into my work. I would regularly get away on trips to other places in Sweden and Europe. I would feel so alive and free when I travelled. I visited the south of Sweden, where my partner's family lived, extensively. Many day walks and weekend trips were made throughout Värmland to national parks and historical sites. When I got away and explored, I felt the life seep back into my veins. I took this and used it to write freelance pieces on travelling in Sweden for travel platforms, and started my own travel blog about my adventures.

However, my day job began to become a constant struggle for me. I was good at what I did — researching, teaching and writing were natural gifts that I excelled at and enjoyed very much. But I was working in a department where I was the only non-Swedish colleague, and where my co-workers were not particularly social. As I didn't have friends outside work, it was important to me that my work environment be a positive one, but I struggled to relate to my colleagues, particularly the Swedish ones. Those I did manage to click with tended to be international PhD students.

I tried to be active and social, and keep busy, but I dreaded entering the *fika* room and making small talk with people and pretending to laugh and understand what they were saying. My colleagues would praise how great my Swedish was, and believed that because I could speak quite well that I understood everything. But I was left incredibly confused on a daily basis, both by simple conversations and in academic discussions about political philosophy in a language that I'd only been using for a couple of years, and it effected my self-confidence.

But the crux of it all was that I wasn't able to be myself. My Swedish was good, but I didn't have the cultural lingo to pick up on jokes or pop culture references, and I found people switched off easily when I talked because it took me so long to say what I wanted to say.

Reading this, these challenges I faced may sound small. And they were. Who hasn't had a stressful or challenging job, experienced difficulties integrating into a new place or struggled to learn a new language? For me, though, these small things piled on top of one another until they became crippling. Added to these was, of course, the fact that for six months of the year it was cold and dark. My partner, born in Russia and having lived in Europe his entire life, was unfazed by this. But for me — born and raised in Sydney where the vitamin D is in huge supply — my body suffered for it in spite of my best efforts.

//

As Michael Booth touches on in *The Almost Nearly Perfect People*, Sweden is not necessarily the Utopia it is made out to be. But for so long I truly believed I was living in a paradise on earth, and that any challenges I faced were trifles. If I was living in the world's happiest country, then I should be happy. Why was I so unhappy?

I kept telling myself that things would get better, and that I would integrate — it would all just take time. But as I hit the two year mark (three years, if you count the year I'd lived there working as an au pair), I decided to do some research. For every survey that tells us that Sweden is the happiest and most equal country in the world, there are statistics that show that things aren't so rosy. Over half of Sweden's households are one person households according to Eurostat — the highest percentage in the entire European Union. That means that a lot of Swedes live alone. With generous childcare benefits, parental leave schemes and free universal education Sweden may seem like a great place to live. In fact, it's regularly rated as one of the top countries to relocate to. But the Internations Expat Insider Survey repeatedly ranks Sweden as one of the worst countries to make friends in. Norway, Denmark and Sweden are the bottom three countries in the 'Finding Friends' subcategory of the 'Ease of Settling in Index'. So I wasn't alone.

I talked with many expats who shared similar feelings. They persisted, too. Some had started a family in Sweden. Others had no choice, as their homes had been devastated by war. I was not in a situation like this; I had a choice. So when someone suggested to me that I could go home — the very first person to even mention that it was a possibility — it was as though a weight had lifted from my shoulders.

I had wanted to return home — or at least to move away from Sweden — for a long time. I just hadn't entertained the idea as a serious possibility. I truly believed that academia was the career for me, even when my work was causing me a lot of frustration and anguish. I believed that I had to stick it out, and keep trying. Even after two years. I thought I was the one who had to compromise, and didn't even consider that there were other options. It was as though I needed another person to tell me that I had a choice in order to realise that I did.

And so, late in 2016, I quit my job, booked a ticket to Auckland and arrived at my cousins' house in rural Auckland. I didn't have a plan, all I knew was that I needed to be in a familiar environment and that I needed to put my life back together.

//

- Cooking *blodpudding* and *pytt i panna* for the first time.
- Experiencing my first -20 Celsius day.
- The point when I realised I could converse in Swedish without assistance.
- When Loreen won Eurovision with 'Euphoria'.
- A motorcycle adventure across the Arctic Circle.
- Gazing upon Viking relics in the south of the country.
- The best yoga classes I have ever been to.

These are among my many fond memories of living in Sweden. Sweden is a happy place and a place of opportunity for so many, and I count myself lucky to have lived and worked there for as long as I did. Living in Sweden taught me to value the simple things in life and to appreciate the sunshine and the outdoors.

While I wouldn't call the time there the best years of my life, they were very much formative years. They gave me time to reflect and discover what it was I truly loved to do: write. I learned what I needed in order to be happy, and to live the sort of life I wanted to lead.

Whenever I see something Swedish — a *dalahäst* on a tea towel design at a craft market, an IKEA importer, a picture on Instagram — I do miss Sweden. I miss its curious culture and mysterious people I could never truly figure out. I miss the fields of Värmland, the scent of the pine forests, and ease of using apps like Swish, which haven't really taken off in this part of the world yet. My laptop that was bought in Sweden still has a Swedish keyboard, and whenever someone else goes to use it and struggles to type the @ sign I remember how I too struggled to master the new orientation and those funny characters that had once looked as unfamiliar to me as they do to my friends here in New Zealand.

I didn't leave Sweden because I didn't like it. I left because I was exhausted and I had nothing more to give. I'd worked hard to become fluent in the language, but so many of the cultural norms eluded me. I'd tried to make friends, but it wasn't easy. I tried my best to get through the long, dark winters, but my Australian-born body craved vitamin D and it was difficult to fight the depression that would resurface every winter.

Neither do I regret moving to Sweden, and living there for as long as I did. It taught me a lot about myself, about what I want and need out of life, and who I am as a person. I will always love the Swedish language. Despite being so isolated, I made friends for life there who I will remain in touch with always. The country itself is beautiful and will always fascinate me. I challenged myself in ways I could not have imagined doing and pulled through. But it was not my place. I tried my hardest to make Sweden my home, but that was the problem. My time there made me realise that you cannot force a connection with a place, just as you cannot force a connection with another person.

/ /

Inhaling the fresh air atop one of Auckland's iconic volcanic domes, I recall for a moment the crispness of the air on a cool autumn day in the Värmland countryside. It's a memory that makes me think of golden fields, pine trees and dark lakes. A landscape that is very different from the one I gaze upon now. One that I will treasure and remember always, but one which is now a part of a past life.

Joshua Bookman

Country of origin: The United States of America.
Profession: Artist.
Current occupation: Looking for a job.
Arrived in Sweden: 2017.
Reason for coming to Sweden: Potential scholarship.
Reason for leaving Sweden: My scholarship application was rejected.

Some reverse American dreams

I walked with Veronica to baggage claim,
collecting her luggage,
and then collecting our train tickets
but my credit card
pin code
'enter your pin code'
the attendant kept demanding
but she stepped in and swiped her credit card
550 SEK

a new train ticket in hand
as we walked through the doors
down the escalators
into the frigid undertunnels
faced by Veronica a woman lost interrupted us

asked for directions

my train arrived

as Veronica was mid-conversation I

interrupted

holding her hand ever so gently —

her fingertips saying it was nice to meet you

her smile lasting

if you'd like find me on Facebook

Bookman, she nodded, memorising and remembering

as I flew back home to Los Angeles my car battery died. I paid $180 to open a rusted grey car door, and then someone nearly ran me over. I ducked back into my car and drove to a sandwich shop, one that serves my favourite butter. It's a 10:00 sunshine butter, the yellow of skies that emerge from early morning smog. I thought of this as I stepped out and into dog shit. I took off my white Nikes and drove immediately back to my apartment, barefoot. I heated leftover coffee and logged onto a low budget travel web site and booked a plane ticket for the cheapest return flight to Europe: Stockholm. Two days later I was at the Arlanda airport. That day, I received an invitation to Konstfack.

This time though, I showed up,

and I knew I wasn't going to clasp her hand.

a new train ticket in pocket as I walked

through the doors

down the escalators

into the frigid undertunnels
faced by Veronica
I had held her arm
this time
I wasn't going to clasp her hand
as I said goodbye
to her
to this July

I needed to prepare for my interview. It was in a week. I sat myself at a coffee shop in Södermalm when I saw a man next to me furiously typing away at his keyboard. He had a stack of three books, one related to financial capital. I remember the walls as pale blue, a playground color for adults. The pastry display was limited, but the sandwich prices reasonable. The whole neighbourhood seemed like the archipelago shorewashed, not busy enough to impose meaning onto. The barista interrupted. 'An espresso, please. *Enkel*.' I stumbled in Swedish, embarrassed, but tried to practise. Better to impress the walls. We had something in common.

We spoke briefly and got onto the subject of my research interests. 'Who's the professor?' he asked. 'Oh, no, it's at Konstfack,' I said. 'You probably don't know him.' At this point the walls' blue and his blonde hair all blended, a sort of overwhelming Easter egg hunt. I clutched my book as one does a bunny plush toy. 'Oh no, no, I work with all the universities. Even the artists,' he said, smiling. 'Thomas,' I said. 'In the

Design department.' 'Oh, Thomas?' he asked. 'He's one of my good friends.' I dropped my book. He reached into his pocket for his phone and texted him. 'I let Thomas know I've just met ya.' He showed me the text. 'It'll be a good interview,' he said. He closed up his laptop and was walking out of the shop. He turned around to speak to me. 'I hope I see you in my office one day,' he said, smiling, sort of saluting me. It felt like a military cemetery inverted. Instead of endless marble headstones, it was just grass planted for new heroic dreams.

The Airbnb I was staying in was never confirmed, so I reached out to Joacim, who I had met in Gothenburg in 2015. 'If the Airbnb doesn't work out and you need a place to stay my daughter's room is free this weekend and you could crash there if you want,' he said. Or in American English, 'yeah dude, just let me know.' Joacim's eyes were strong. His whole body felt absorbed by the extreme seasons of light, like he was always holding an old leather briefcase and a bottle of easy white wine, a vintage winter and a summer that was just pressed by gleeful grape feet.

I met most of Joacim's family. There was a big family dinner and then a lunch of sorts at Pelikan. His uncle treated me to salted smoked mackerel, and reindeer. Through Joacim I met Maja, who reminded me of Maria, who I had met this past summer. She had hosted me in the best way possible: with smiles, and food.

Maja let me stay with her. 'My boyfriend is just trying to get me to sleep over,' she said, laughing. She was tidying up her apartment for me. She was fixing her bed when I stepped towards the kitchen. I noticed these black and gold teacups. I flipped them over. Made in the USSR. 'Make yourself at home.'

I walked her towards the bike path,
she was off to work
'You shouldn't be so polite'
she smiled,
mid-mother mid-sister mid-friend
'wander down that way'

off she left,
I clutched the white velvet bunny,
the backpack straps
its floppy ears,
and all of their eyes

it wasn't the prettiest path
but each little plaza
of brick and green
of long black coats
and coupled friends

apartments
brick and green
and benches
sinuous and superscribed
Stockholm's islands

the dip into Lidingö's lake
wolf hounds barking at me
I just wanted to pet them
barking furiously
I slipped into the lake
freezing
smiling
I sat on the bench
flippity floppity
hippity hoppity
a siren statue inscribed
for when I decided to return
and imbed
sense into all the cities' cultures I've adopted
Rome into Boston's Swedish kind of California
pin code
'enter your pin code'

3. Expectations

Sweden is known to be a society embracing equal values and opportunities, a place where women and men are on par, where work and life is not in conflict, where pragmatism goes before principle. The working population is known for its excellent English language skills and willingness to turn global. Settling should be easy, smooth and resulting in a better life.

However, the personal journey of integrating new values is much more complex than agreeing with them on paper. There are new angles to discover, consequences never thought of, and the sudden discovery that you might have adapted more than you realised.

This experience also opens up for identifying larger-scale issues, that show a social structure not as perfect as its image, and that Sweden, like any country, has its pros and cons, challenges and opportunities, myths and realities.

3

Me, a feminist, too
Maddy Savage

Mother of all let downs
Jill Leckie

Photo Credit: Anna Gustafsson

Maddy Savage

Country of origin: UK.
Profession: Journalist and presenter.
Current occupation: Freelance journalist for media including BBC, NPR, Monocle and Time Out. I have also produced and hosted the Stockholmer Podcast.
Arrived in Sweden: 2014.
Reason for coming to Sweden: I fell in love with Sweden while visiting and I initially relocated to take a job as the editor of The Local Sweden.
Reason for staying in Sweden: I love having my base in a capital city that's so close to nature. I have been able to grow and diversify my skills thanks to access to Stockholm's start-up ecosystem. Global media are increasingly keen on commissioning news reports from the country.

Me, a feminist, too

The e-mail came during a hurried lunch break, while I was in the midst of one of the most horrific cases of my 15-year career as a journalist. Kim Wall, a fellow freelance reporter from Sweden who was only a few years younger than myself, had died several months earlier after boarding a submarine to interview the Danish inventor Peter Madsen. His murder trial had just got under way. I was covering the story from Copenhagen for the British media.

As I put aside my classically-Danish, salmon-topped open sandwich and clicked on the message, I was expecting it to be a request for yet another live interview — I'd been up since 5 a.m. giving analysis and updates to different TV channels and radio shows. I knew the sender's name — we'd done shifts together in a London newsroom about seven years earlier. But our professional paths hadn't crossed since and we hadn't kept in touch on social media.

'I wondered who that stunning Swedish blonde was on the telly! It was you! You're looking the part!' it read. My stomach lurched. This did not feel appropriate. The writer was old enough to be my father and has a daughter my own age. I'm British, but there's no doubt in my mind that my Swedish female friends would not have been impressed by his stereotyping of their looks.

The timing was also crucial. It was early 2018, just months after the Me Too movement gained attention. I was covering a murder trial involving the mutilation of a female journalist. It was -7 Celsius and I was wearing a functional thick down jacket. This wasn't the kind of story I wanted to look glamorous for. And if there was any time of the year when a male colleague should have been aware of his words, it was this one. March 8th. International Women's Day. I swiftly finished my sandwich, but was left with a bitter taste.

Sexual harassment and sexism comes in many forms, and I'm well aware that this was a minor incident. But for me personally, getting that e-mail was something of an awakening. I realised that during the four years I'd spent in Stockholm, not once had I experienced this kind of everyday sexism. I can't say exactly how often it took place during my career in the UK, but I guess there's a reason the Everyday Sexism Project started there.

I swiftly decided to send a response to my former colleague, explaining why I'd felt uncomfortable. I was, of course, inspired by the Me Too movement, but, perhaps more significantly to me personally, I felt empowered by the fact that calling out a senior, older, male colleague was something I would have struggled with before I moved to Sweden. Not anymore.

It was 2014 when I relocated to the Swedish capital, initially to take a job as the editor of the country's largest English-language newspaper, The Local Sweden. I knew the Nordic country was a place famous for feminist and family-friendly policies. But to be honest, I was much more attracted to its pinch-yourself natural beauty, minimalist furniture and innovative start-up scene than its parental leave system. I was a single, childless woman in my early thirties.

But I quickly realised that Sweden's gender equality efforts can have far wider implications than just making it easier for both parents to work. When sharing childcare more equally starts to become normalised (thanks to affordable day care and generous parental leave for mothers and fathers), so does the idea of having a balance of men and women in senior jobs, regardless of whether or not they have kids. And with that comes a greater respect for women from society as a whole.

The first example came the night I arrived in Sweden and watched the evening news with my new flatmate. It didn't matter that I didn't understand a word. I was immediately impressed that there was a more equal representation of female journalists on screen. The bulletin also drew attention to the female leaders at the helm of numerous political parties. Even women's show jumping led the sports section of the show.

In the months that followed, I was highly impressed by the growing numbers of female entrepreneurs — of all ages — that I came across through my work and at networking events. Perhaps also connected to Sweden's famously flat business structures, this was a community that felt open, collaborative and far less competitive than similar groupings I had come across in London. Moreover, my conversations with other women seemed to focus on our future possibilities, rather than the 'struggles' of being a female working in the media or business.

I was enjoying my managerial role at The Local Sweden, but I had always dreamt of being a freelance reporter out in the field and becoming my own boss. Feeling that I would be guaranteed support from other entrepreneurs in Stockholm — both female and male, I quit my job as an editor after 18 months in the role and set myself up as a sole trader at the age of 34.

All this was a huge contrast to the ten years I spent working as a reporter in the British media. I lost count of the number of times I was told — by both men and women — how hard it would be to continue a journalism career as I got older, given the often erratic hours. It was usually assumed both that I would want children and that I would become their primary caregiver. I spent most of my twenties racing to get as far ahead as possible, so that I'd either be able to tick off my key reporting goals before 'settling down' and going part-time, or have a fighting chance of returning to work after maternity leave at a similar level. Over the last four years, not one person in Sweden has commented on my gender in relation to my job. Working in this environment has made me more confident, more independent and much more ready to navigate issues such as pay negotiations, gender imbalance within projects I work on and, of course, sexist e-mails.

I haven't had children and it's not a priority for me right now. But with free IVF available to single mothers in Sweden, generous parental leave and subsidised day care (or night care for shift workers), having a child — even alone — is a possibility that might not stand in the way of my career progression. Not only would I potentially find it easier to continue working full-time in journalism than it might have been in the UK, I think there would be much less judgement from the wider society about me being a single parent (or, alternatively, splitting childcare responsibilities equally with my partner), than there might be in many other parts of the world.

On the other hand, working in Stockholm, which has one of the highest proportions of single-person households in the EU (in part, linked to a 50 percent divorce rate), means I can easily access a fulfilling social life with people of my own age. This actually makes me feel less pressured to rush into having my own biological children, just because my clock is ticking or because that's what might have been expected of me within my friendship circle and professional network back in the UK.

Sweden is by no means perfect when it comes to gender equality and it's important to point out that while it does offer a more progressive environment for women than many other parts of the world, it is not a Utopia. In 2016, more than 80% of managers at listed Swedish companies were men and not a single new business on the stock market had a woman boss. Meanwhile, it's still much more common for parents who work part time to be mothers, rather than fathers. A gender pay gap remains here too.

Sweden has not completely stamped out sexism and sexual offences either — just weeks after the covering the Kim Wall murder trial, I was reporting for global media about multiple allegations concerning an arts profile linked to the Swedish Academy which awards the annual Nobel Literature Prize. The surrounding drama lead to the postponement of the prize in 2018.

Yet despite these cracks in Sweden's glowing global image, for me, there is still a marked cultural difference between Sweden and the UK when it comes to attitudes towards women. I personally feel I have so much more freedom as a woman living in Stockholm than I ever did in London. I feel more comfortable calling out discrimination when I notice it, and I feel privileged that I am lucky enough to be living in such a gender-aware society.

So what happened with that e-mail?

Well, times are slowly changing in the UK. The man in question responded to my message later that day, apologising for causing me any discomfort: 'It was ill judged, though only meant to be pleasant and well-meaning,' he wrote. 'I really meant nothing untoward, and am sorry it came out that way.'

That is the problem with a lot of everyday sexism. The offenders simply don't know what they are doing or what the ramifications might be. But after living and working in Sweden for four years, I do.

If I wasn't a feminist before I moved here, I certainly am now.

Jill Leckie

Country of origin: Scotland.
Profession and occupation: Founder and editor of
Littlebearabroad.com #StockholmforKids, podcaster and
writer. Founder of The International Parent Integration
Project Stockholm.
Arrived in Sweden: 2015.
Reason for coming to Sweden: *Kärleksinvandrare.*
Reason for staying in Sweden: Both my *sambo* and
daughter are Swedish and I want to live with them.

Mother of all let downs

My Swedish career started with a knock-back. I suppose they all do, don't they? The sudden realisation that finding a job in Sweden, whilst pregnant and without having learnt Swedish, was never going to happen. To say that I had been led up the garden path and around the back of the house was an understatement when it came to my expectations of returning to work in Sweden. My *sambo*'s family had been absolute in their assurances that I would find a job in no time, but the gaping hole between my expectations and their definition of a job was, let's say, an abyss.

How many times has someone said to you: 'You'll get a job in no time!', 'It's easy. You speak English, you'll be hired in a few months.' Well, no! It doesn't work like that and I think it's about time that we (the transient, international, working immigrant community) all start talking about that. This is especially the case when it comes to female spouses, who make up 84% of accompanying spouses (InterNations 2015 Expat Spouse Survey). So, let's deal with the clamour of 'sexism' immediately and underline that re-entering the workforce in a foreign country, as a spouse, is a proportionately female dilemma.

I'm a believer in setting the tone. I know I speak from a place of privilege; that is not going to stop me from saying that there is a deeply hidden undercurrent of discrimination in the Swedish labour market against foreign-born women.

What's your point?

Sweden is still a politically socialist society, at its core, despite what some may think. Born out of 'The Nordic model' of social and economic policies of universal welfare built partly thanks to high taxation and free market capitalism, there is deep outrage at the slightest notion of intolerance, inequality or restricting someone's right to adequate assistance. However, this only goes so far. For the average female, international, working immigrant, don't expect much in the way of outrage on your behalf. Which is fine, quite rightly; there are others so much worse off than that demographic.

The first problem for female, international, English-speaking immigrants are our expectations. Most of us arrive in Sweden with expectations of an easy-life just because we speak English and we're often given this false hope by those already living in Sweden. When I moved to Sweden, I was the operations manager of a multi-million pound, multi-venue conferencing and meeting business in central London. However, it quickly became clear that I was not 'employable' in the eyes of a Swedish company. I had no 'hard skills', no 'technical proficiency' or 'industry qualifications' and I didn't speak Swedish, at all. So, regardless of 15 years of experience at the top of my industry, I was worthless. Less than worthless, I was a nuisance. It felt like overnight I had gone from an intelligent, resourceful business woman to living on the fringes of society.

The funny thing was that this didn't seem to be happening to the dads that I had met at playgroup who were in the same position. They seemed to be walking into jobs with relative ease, regardless of their proficiency in Swedish. Was it because I was a new mum? Was it my age? Was it because I was a woman? Or was it simply because the industries that most men find themselves in (IT, gaming, software development, pharma, finance, management consultancy) were, ironically, less discriminatory when it came to language proficiency and more interested in your industry experience. Was it the classic old boys club? Men who can't speak Swedish are just doing their best. Women who can't speak Swedish are just annoying? I still haven't found the answer to this mystery. Answers on a postcard anyone!

What angered me even more was the presumption that women should just take what's offered to them. An officer at *Arbetsförmedlingen* once told me that Sweden needed more carers, so I should go and look after a bunch of elderly people. Why? Because I'm a woman? Because my only useful, pre-determined skill from society's point of view is caring? Trust me, those elderly people do not want me looking after them anymore than I want to be doing it. Why should I, a person with a graduate degree and almost 15 years of experience at the top of my industry, have to throw in the towel on a career that took time and money to nurture? And there it was, the eventual plummet down the rabbit hole of cultural alienation and failure to integrate as an immigrant, isolation and the obvious implosion of self-confidence. Thanks *Arbetsförmedlingen*. Put that in your pipe and smoke it Ulf Kristersson.

The proof

In 2007, a study was published called 'What's in a Name' by Moa Brusell. It was a field experiment for the existence of foreign-born or ethnic discrimination in the hiring process in Sweden. The study found evidence of extensive ethnic discrimination of both men and women in the Swedish labour market. In February 2017, Sweden received a warning from the Organisation for Economic Co-operation and Development (OECD): 'Special attention should be paid to the integration of foreign-born women, who are particularly lagging behind.' *TCO Sverige*, the Swedish Confederation for Professional Employees, has acknowledged the crisis facing Sweden and how it treats foreign-born women in the labour market.

At a recent seminar that I attended, hosted by *TCO Sverige*, with a panel from the Swedish Government, the lobbyist party *Kvinna till Kvinna*, *Arbetsförmedlingen* and union representatives, there was agreement across the panel that too much public focus and media attention had been placed on getting foreign-born men into the Swedish labour market to prevent 'deviance' (I kid you not), and that foreign-born women had simply been forgotten. Once again women are side-lined, inadvertently, because of male deviance. Oh Mary! The irony.

Right now, a thorough examination of the Swedish labour market and the discrimination of foreign-born women needs to be carried out. Is anyone to blame? The government, the employers, society's view of foreign-born women, the foreign-born women themselves, cultural values, discrimination...; the list could go on and on.

Is it useful at the end of the day to assign blame? Not really. But action needs to be taken and the discussion needs to be in a positive and open manner. There has been recognition by certain parties that attitudes need to be changed. However, I fear that over the next 12 months, Sweden will shift its immigration policy and integration strategies to reflect that of many other European countries: becoming insular and more isolated to appease the increasingly right-wing, conservative attitudes on the rise.

It's not all doom and gloom

You'd be forgiven for wondering what the hell this depressing and doomsday account of starting a career in Sweden was. However, I think it's my responsibility, and the responsibility of others like me, to be honest and give a full account of the reality of building a life in Sweden. In the last 10 years, Sweden has become less tolerant. By that I mean that the Swedish way of life is being challenged and it scares the crap out of them. One in six people living in Sweden were born outside the country according to Statistics Sweden's (*SCB*) survey from 2015. Like many societies and cultures that feel threatened by immigration, Sweden is becoming more inward-looking, desperate to protect its culture and traditions. Even political rhetoric from the moderates is more insular, more nationalistic.

As much as Sweden ticks the boxes on a number of levels and appears far more advanced than most European/international countries, socially, there's a segment of society that keeps getting missed: foreign-born women, especially mothers: a subject close to my heart. At every stage of the integration process which Sweden has carefully crafted for its newly-arrived immigrants, mothers are continuously let down. No more so than in the process of learning the Swedish language and job-hunting. How does one solve the problem of getting women work-ready, in a foreign country, whilst caring for children? There are band-aid initiatives that claim to solve this issue but, in reality, they are more cosmetic than cure.

I can only speak for myself when I say that I was not prepared to sit around and wait to be deemed work-ready in the eyes of somebody else (read, the state). And if nobody else was going to employ me, I would just employ myself. It's a choice that many, many foreign-born mothers turn to. Not content with being told when and where they could work or relying on public services to assist them, foreign-born mothers are creating their own opportunities. The rise of the female 'parentrepreneur' goes on, facilitated by social media, digital advancements in building and curating web-shops and private, online training. If you know where to look, you can access some amazing initiatives for female entrepreneurs in Sweden. My favourites are:

- **SHE Entrepreneurs:** an initiative for MENA born women living in Sweden
- **WEgate:** the European Commission's gateway to women's entrepreneurship.
- **Open up!** A National Strategy for Business Promotion on Equal Terms 2015-2020.

I started my own business, Littlebearabroad, for the reasons above. And the desperate search for straightforward advice that didn't come from some total stranger that had no idea about my personal circumstances and lurked in online forums. But mostly because I saw a huge opportunity to create a totally unique platform for international parents living in Sweden that didn't have a bloody clue what was going on and had nowhere to turn.

Happily, in the course of my entrepreneurial journey, I've met dozens of women in exactly the same situation as me. All choosing to take the risk of starting their own hustles instead of pandering to the shaky labour market and shoddy internal workings of Swedish HR policies. I'm a member of brilliant networks for female entrepreneurs specialising in parent-focused businesses and She-led businesses.

In March 2017, I set up MamaMötet, a female-focused business network for international mothers establishing their own hustles in Stockholm. Its sole purpose is to provide a platform for international mother's to meet like-minded mothers and establish those crucial networks that lead to furthering their ambitions in business. But you don't have to have your own business. There's an argument that you have an even greater need to establish these networks when you're looking for a job. After all, it's not what you know, it's who you know in Sweden.

The Swede life

My career journey in Sweden has barely started. We're a micro business that has mega plans and it's going to take time to see them come to fruition. But, had it not been for the challenges I faced in coming to terms with the fact that my employment status was pretty much void once I moved abroad, I wouldn't have even dreamt of starting my own business. I would encourage any woman, especially mothers moving abroad, to consider holding their nose and diving into starting their own business. Pushing back against being told when you are deemed fit to work (read, Swedish enough) and taking the proverbial bawbag by the horns to make it work for you seems like a much healthier alternative than putting your life on hold.

But, of course, that's just me. I've developed a serious distaste for authority in the last couple of years. I think it has something to do with the feelings of ineptitude brought about by some of the less pleasant characteristics of the Swedish psyche. But, that's a whole other book in itself.

Ironically, I actually do love living in Sweden. I know, you're probably staring at that sentence with one eyebrow raised. It probably seems like I've been Sweden-bashing for the majority of this chapter but I really do love Sweden. It's an incredibly advanced society and the work done on behalf of gender equality and equal rights is immense compared to other countries. When I return to my home country, I'm horrified at the venom you still see and hear in the media, in the streets and even from family members about gender issues and equality. How Sweden treats women is miles ahead but, as I said before, it's not perfect and change needs to happen to prevent a looming crisis of foreign-born female unemployment.

Lastly, I would like to add that the lack of statistics, evidence and research carried out on the status of unemployment amongst foreign-born women, especially mothers, is appalling. There is a concerning gap in the data-sets of the research on unemployment figures and entrepreneurism when it comes to foreign-born female entrepreneurs. Perhaps this is indicative of the cultural and social climate we've been living in for the last millennia?

4. Eyes of others

Being invited to a job interview, getting a new job, collaborating with others; all of this depends on others recognising who we are and what we can do. In our home countries, where cues and attributes are appreciated according to a similar framework, this is rarely noticeable. However, in a new environment, the eyes of others will not look at us in the same way.

Our identity, unquestionably, is affected by this. As the others turn into a new group of people – another society, this view changes, and we might question our integrity, self-worth and, in practice, employability. Are we merely a series of reflections, all mirroring each other and our ambitions, needs and desires just to fit in with the masses and please them?

4

Subject: (No subject)
Franziska Müller

Trust score
Raman Ramalingam

The fourth reflection or the broken mirror
Werner Renck

Photo Credits: Morten Falch Sortland

Franziska Müller

Country of origin: Germany.
Profession and current occupation: Implementing innovative human resource management concepts and solutions which are based on theory and work in practice.
Arrived in Sweden: 28 August 2014.
Reason for coming to (and staying in) Sweden: I came for my studies and to do ancestry research (that has now been completed).

Subject: (No subject)

When they decide to move on with other candidates.[1]
When your application is rejected within two hours and eight minutes.[2]
When you have to have a little bit extra to offer.[3]
When the subject and your name are undercover.[4]
When the interest for this employment has been significant.[5]
When there are specific requirements to meet.[6]
When you didn't pick the longest straw this time.[7]
When the role has been put on hold and then cancelled.[8]
When you encounter some language confusion.[9]
When you don't receive an answer at all.[10]

1: **Subject: Regarding the position as**
████████████████████████

19 Oct 2015, 09:00

Dear Franziska,

Concerning your application for the
position as ████████████████████████.

We have got many qualified applications
and we have decided to move on with
other candidates in this recruitment
process.

Thank you for your interest in our
company and we hope you keep an eye on
our career page for new vacancies!

Kind Regards,

████████████████

████████████

████████████████████████████

2: **Subject: Your application for** ████████
████████████████████████

10 Dec 2015 13:40

Dear Franziska,
Thanks for your interest in ████████!
We have received your application for
the following position: ████████████████
████████████████.
What happens next? If your skills and
experience are a strong match for the
role, a member of our team will reach
out to you to schedule some time for
conversation. In the meantime, feel free
to learn more about careers at ████████
by visiting https://www.████████████
████████████/careers.

Subject: Your application for ████████
████████████████████████

10 Dec 2015 15:48

Dear Franziska,

Thank you for your interest in the
████████████████████████████
position at ████████. At this time, we
have decided not to move forward with
your application

Please feel free to learn about other
opportunities at ████████ by visiting
https://www.████████████████████
████████/careers.

Best of luck for the future.

3: **Subject:** ███████████████████████
26 Feb 2016

Dear Franziska,

Thank you for your e-mail. Since we have
received more than 400 applications for
the position, we are unfortunately not
able to give personal feedback. There
have been many qualified candidates why
we have moved forward with those who
had a little bit extra to offer for the
concrete positions.

I hope that this answer will help you.
Otherwise you are welcome to call me.

4: **Subject:(No subject)**
17 Jun 2016 11:31

Dear Applicant,

Thank you for your recent application
with ████████.

Unfortunately, having now reviewed all
applications, we have decided not to
progress your application any further.
Although you have an interesting profile,
this is because we felt other candidates
were a closer fit to the role profile.

We would like to thank you for the time
you have invested in the recruitment
process and for your patience in
awaiting the outcome.

Should you see any other roles in the
future that you feel your skills and
experience might be suited to, we would
be happy to receive an application from
you.

5: **Subject: Regarding your application for** ███████████████████████████ **at** ████████
30 May 2016

Dear Sir / Madam,

Thank you for your application as
████████'s ████████████████████████████!
The interest for this employment has
been significant and we have received
incredibly impressive applications.

Unfortunately, we have now decided to
continue the recruitment process with
someone else. Once more, we are very
thankful for your application and hope
you can continue to review our website
for future job adds.

6: **Subject:** ███████████
9 May 2016

Hi Franziska,
Thank you for writing. Glad to hear you are interested in ███████!

It is a tough question to answer, as you can understand I cannot guarantee anything. One prerequisites is a high level of Swedish as the program will be held in Swedish. Another one is that you should preferably be in your last year of your masters in engineering or economics.

If you meet these requirements I would recommend you to apply.

Kind Regards,
███████████

7:    **Subject: Update on job application @** ██████████

8 January 2017 11:38

Hi, first of all I want to say that I'm very happy about your interest for ████████████ @ ██████. I know that sending an application takes small moments of preparations, and I do really appreciate it. Unfortunately, you didn't pick the longest straw this time.

Why didn't I, you might ask yourself. Well, sometimes it's not a match and the right position is out there for you, and I would be super happy if you keep an eye on our job board for future openings.

Best Regards,
████████

8:      **Subject:(No subject)**
31 May 2017

Dear Franziska,

Thank you for your enquiry. Having
looked into this I can see that the
role you have applied for was put on
hold and then cancelled, so we did not
ultimately hire anyone for the ██ ████
████ position.

Thank you for your interest in ███ and
good luck in your search for a new role.

Best Regards,
████

9: **Subject: Vielen Dank für Ihre Bewerbung**
29 Nov 2017

Thank you for your interest in working for ████. We appreciate the time you have taken to submit your application.

At this time, we have decided to move forward with other candidates whose qualifications satisfy the minimum requirements of the position. However, we will keep your resume/CV in our current file for consideration should a suitable vacancy arise. We also invite you to any additional opportunities within ████ that interest you.

We wish you every success in your career endeavours!

Once on the ████████ home page this task can be accessed by clicking on the "Message Center" in the upper right corner of the screen, (Round circle with number in it). This task can also be viewed when accessing your Inbox within ████.

If you are logged into ████████'s network, and you are a L-████████ employee, please click:

████████████████████

Wenn Sie im ████████ -Netzwerk angemeldet und ein Legacy ████████- Mitarbeiter sind, klicken Sie bitte auf:

████████████████████

Wenn Sie nich im Netzwerk angemeldet
sind, klicken Sie auf:

████████████████████████████████

Wenn Sie Fragen zu dieser
Baenachrichtgung haben, wenden Sie sich
bitte an ██████████ über den Contact
Us-Link, den Sie bei den obigen Links
finden.

10:

Raman Ramalingam

Country of origin: India.
Profession and current occupation: Head of talent.
Arrived in Sweden: 2010.
Reason for coming to Sweden: I came to Sweden to pursue my master of science degree because the finest technological education was offered for free even for non-European Union citizens.

Trust score

A search in *allabolag.se* (a search service for Swedish companies) with '*rekrytering*' (the Swedish word for recruiting) and 'Stockholm' gives 1225 results. One of the most common questions I receive from the expat community is this: 'With so many recruitment firms in Stockholm, why am I still struggling to find a job?'

The answer to this question explains the gap into which foreign talent often falls. Let's break the recruitment process into its three basic segments:

1) **Talent acquisition:** Acquiring/finding relevant talents.
2) **Validation:** Analysing, testing and examining the skills and personality of the talent.
3) **Hiring:** Agreeing on the conditions and offer to sign the contract.

Obviously every company that is recruiting invests a considerable amount of effort to talent acquisition since that's what they are after.

'But how does international talent get missed out of this talent search?'

Well, the answer to that question lies in the second phase of the recruitment process: validation. There's no surprise here really. Most of the validation happens over a stringent interview process with several levels of face-to-face conversations (which may also include occasional case analyses, workshops or sample project deliveries).

The real question to explore is: 'How does one get selected for an interview?'

That depends on (what I'd like to call) your 'trust score'. Calculating your trust score basically involves analysing each and every keyword in your résumé and mapping it against the relevance it holds in the local market (the local market in this example is Sweden). The two main parameters involved in calculating trust scores are:

Brands: The brand of your associated university, company and organizations/groups.

Networks: Your friends, colleagues, clients, acquaintances and basically every person you are connected with.

Taking Sweden as an example, imagine a person born and raised here. Naturally, this person would score high on the trust score compared to his or her foreign alternatives because every connection or brand this person associates with, has a greater probability to carrying a higher trust score in the local market.

To quote a simple example: the Stockholm School of Economics would have a considerably greater trust value in Sweden as a brand compared to the Católica Lisbon School of Business and Economics (Portugal), even though, according to the recent Financial Times business school report, they share similar overall rankings.

Thus, when you are a candidate from abroad, calculation of this trust score is tricky since universities, companies and networks are harder to validate in the context of the local market, as the recruiters have limited knowledge of them. This problem is also experienced by Swedes who've worked abroad for many years and come back home realising how difficult it is for them to land their next job. This highlights the need for an external and more structured validation mechanism in Sweden and the Nordics that will not only open doors for refugee talent to the job market, but, also make Sweden more attractive for international talent.

This is a revised version of an article that was originally published on Medium, 3rd of April 2016.

Werner Renck

Country of origin: Chile.
Profession and current occupation: Architect.
Arrived in Sweden: 2011.
Reason for coming to Sweden: My wife is Swedish and we lived eight years together before moving here. We were living in Chile with our two daughters, but it was difficult to reconcile work and family. For this reason we decided to change to my wife's country and thus start everything again.
Reason for staying in Sweden: I don´t think there is a better place for my daughters, so this is my place with them.

The fourth reflection or the broken mirror

Belatedly he will realise that this invitation for a coffee outside the office was actually an apology for what was to come.

The whole situation has been full of apparent contrasts. He is not so dark-skinned, but next to her, he is. She uses fluent and nice words and manners; he is straight and rough, rather out of necessity than by features of his personality.

He is facing a view of those who might be going to similar appointments, or not, and he clearly recognises them. She is sitting in front of him looking outside, at the blurry and shaking colours of the people in a rainy afternoon visible through the large window behind him. Well, he drinks an espresso and she doesn't.

They both look at each other like they already know what they will hear and say. It's there from the very beginning; the meaningless purpose of this meeting. In short, she is very nice, neither is he.

It's like two mirrors, one in front of the other. It's this kind of impenetrable glass, the end and the beginning of that impossible space, inhabited by nothing but reflections.

Perhaps he has Tranströmer in mind when he writes that it's the mirror that looks at him and not him at the mirror, as he would tend to think — if he had thought about it, of course. Surely from repeating the text so often Tranströmer appears from time to time, without reflecting, his words just appear.

'Inom mig bär jag mina tidigare ansikten,
som ett träd har sina årsringar.
Det är summan av dem som är 'jag'.
Spegeln ser bara mitt senaste ansikte,
jag känner av mina tidigare.'

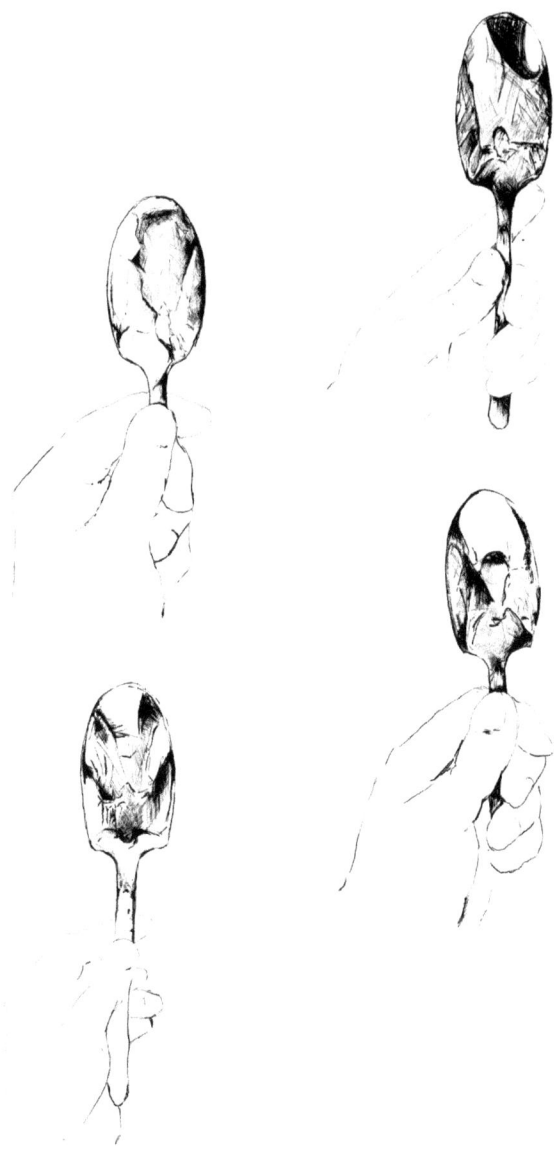

Learning to understand those lines was his first personal achievement when he seriously embarked — in his own way — on learning the new language. Well, of course, to understand it literally, only word for word, like a melody that needs no more than itself.

I think that this text should be somehow involved in their discussion, because the questions in these kinds of circumstances are often sneaky: who looks at whom, who is the one reflected. Is this also the secret that will make him realise that new relationships that are established — or realise new relationships? Only these veiled questions relieve the annoyance of that initial understanding of the verse. That annoyance, which at times is disappointment and, at others, rage, that the time in him a sum of 'Is', as annual rings in a tree. An image that he, of course, doesn't share.

Oddly, she fills one of the uncomfortable seconds of silence. 'It's time to round off, I guess it should say according to the protocol,' she says with a sure tone and with a gesture as if she were telling herself, as if she has come up with *the* answer. 'You have had bad luck,' followed by — but with another tone — 'Nothing is forever.' A comforting sound more meaningful to her than to him.

Bad luck!? You could read the expression on his face. And he doesn't say anything.

He doesn't say anything; it's like a bowl of cold water both because of the apparent banality of the assertion, as for what is triggered in his world of associations.

Bad luck!? He has just begun his seventh year; the seventh year of penance according to the superstition of the broken mirror.

He stands up and, for a moment, he goes behind his gaze, outward, almost turning inside out. He is able to see himself as a third person, both a stranger and a familiar guy talking with one another. It's at that minute that he recognizes their looks. The kind of look that only the initiated — or indoctrinated as others would say — could recognize instinctively. The look that allows them to make a pact, perhaps *the* pact. The pact of oblivion. Maybe this is how everything can be re-done in a different way.

5. Making sense

The process of turning the unfamiliar into the familiar is also a process of no longer noticing the fragments of culture that make up the new. Another, perhaps bigger, picture emerges. At the same time, we might be faced with the no-longer adventurous being in the new place, leaving us with the options of accepting ourselves as blending into that picture, or continue exploring, scratching the surfaces of the everyday, finding new angles and new sources of light.

Sometimes, we might not find purpose with our pursuits until we stop looking for it. Life rarely turns out according to the plan, but this doesn't necessarily mean that our efforts have been wasted. Only from a distance does it make sense.

5

Naked so what
Federica Viero

Untitled
Olga Talalay

A departure is the arrival to someplace new
Veronika Opatřilová

Federica Viero

Countries of origin: Italy, France.
Profession and current occupation Organisational
consultant, intercultural training specialist, designer and
facilitator of learning experiences.
Arrived in Sweden: 2014.
Reason for coming to Sweden: I moved to Sweden as a
result of the conjunction between two factors: my quest for
new growth and new challenges in my professional life and
a Sweden-based job offered to my significant other.
Reason for staying in Sweden: I feel I have meaningful work
to complete here and some promising things to explore, so
I'm staying.

Naked so what

Do you like puzzles? I mean real puzzles, no metaphors just yet. Landscapes, city skylines. A puzzle is when you've been assuming for hours — or days — that the choppy water off the coast, past the harbour, is where that greyish piece belongs, only to realise in the end — and with great amusement — that in fact that blasted piece of grey is nothing but a blurry detail in the façade of the administrative building in the foreground.

When I moved to Sweden four years ago, I had no idea I was about to tackle the most captivating puzzle I had ever dealt with by far. It wasn't even my first international relocation, and still I feel like the ongoing journey I embarked on was very much like the process of composing a beautiful, complex puzzle. All the aspects are there, indeed: the curiosity, the doubts, the inquiries, the guesses, the mistakes, the motivational ups and downs, and then the learning, the small wins, the amazement.

A puzzle can string you along and make you turn around in circles for a while before offering you a stunning perspective that you would have hardly imagined possible, and so can an expatriation. Would you enjoy starting such a journey led by your curiosity, being proved wrong by your own steps and growing wiser along the way?

If you are like me, you would then find yourself making avid observations along the way, and guesses after a while. Some of them would likely turn out to be near misses. For example, when I assumed that the reason there were fully-equipped kitchens in many Swedish offices was because of the habit of embracing the long hours spent at work, seeing the office as a second home.

I tried not to let my guesswork settle into beliefs and went on collecting, taking mental notes, reading research and listening to opinions, until I felt I had to review all these isolated, diverse puzzle pieces. I still try to make sense of them as a whole, looking for patterns, for underlying ideas or facts that could eventually help me figure out the broader picture. For sure, all these noticeable things I have been observing are linked somehow.

Four years into this journey today, while I wouldn't say the big puzzle is completed — it will most likely never be, I do begin to see some form emerging. My personal take on the workplace and business culture, the Swedish way, is taking shape.

One experience that has definitely helped me identify some trends in this picture is my transition from employee to business owner. Interacting with different people every day, and attending all sorts of events, meetings, chats and gatherings has allowed me to become almost serious in my observations, now reaching a somewhat representative sample. That's how, in my perception, quite a few patterns have progressively emerged as being typical Swedish traits.

Unwind

My Italian friend Anna visited me recently. She was intrigued to learn that I was starting my own company. We were sitting in a cosy *konditori* in central Malmö and she was devouring my stories about how I had gone about it. As a chartered legal professional, she was eager to compare styles and processes.

'...and the tax office! I went there last week,' I told Anna.

'You're just starting out, what kind of tax issues did they find? What did they want,' she countered.

'You start a company, you get invited to information meetings on all kind of tax-related topics.'

'Mmm... tax consultants must hate them for giving you access to the holy grail of tax knowledge.'

I explained, 'Well, they are not such a powerful elite here, but what surprised me was our presenters. I was expecting a tough start followed by a darting briefing through dozens of slides. We started with ten minutes housekeeping instructions instead: time schedule, material, toilets, security directions, how to step outside the building for fresh air during the break. A few experts from other organizations that support businesses were also attending, in case we had peripheral questions they were better placed to answer.'

'Oh! Did they pay you attendance fees while they were at it?' 'They didn't, but they let us know that a choice of refreshments would be served in the adjacent coffee space during the break and that they needed to know how many of us were gluten intolerant.'

Move

Let's rewind to my very last working day within a corporate team, just before taking the big leap and going self-employed. It was a Swedish team at a local bank branch. We were having our last *vetelängd*, berries, cheese and coffee together, sitting around our big kitchen table. *Fika* is one of the most widespread and typical Swedish workplace habits. Teams take the time to pause together, having coffee, sweets and fruit, at least once a day. Sometimes twice.

In our team we used to have a special, longer *fika* on Thursday afternoons, with rotating shifts for the shopping and the dishwasher. I was presented with some small gifts and, of course, was asked about my plans for the future. How would I go about it? Where would I start?

I explained: 'One thing I need to decide very soon is whether I should register a sole proprietorship or form a limited company. My personal responsibility is protected with a limited company, but there are more obligations to be aware of. What would you guys say?'

Anders, a customer advisor for private individuals, lifted a finger. 'Well, for example, if you start a limited company, which is separate from your own individual identity, then you'll be able to hire yourself, become a salaried worker and, as such, you'll be entitled to benefit from the *friskvårdsbidrag* (health maintenance allowance) that you as a company will grant to you as an individual. Your company will then have a deductible cost and you will pay much less for your gym card.'

This is a benefit the majority of companies provide to their employees. It's a sort of yearly voucher that the employees can spend on any type of fitness activities. To me it was minutiae, compared to the crucial economic consequences associated with the choice. Still, Anders' tone was not ironic, he was making an important point, somehow.

Breathe

Back in my first days as an employee on Swedish soil, I was navigating the financial department of a large IT company, lost in translation amidst a cheerful crew of colleagues representing as many as 15 different nationalities. By then largely internationalized, the company had nonetheless an authentic Swedish heritage. The local management was mainly Swedish.

My multicultural colleagues and I were struggling with the odds and vagaries of our first financial quarter closing. It was feeling a bit hectic, to say at least. Lunchtime came, on the very last day of the quarter. I had always been told that lunch break at the typical Swedish office was usually kept simple and fairly short, rarely including high-street restaurants, multiple courses, let alone alcohol, and that was clearly the trend we were observing.

So, as soon as we had finished with our plates, we hurried out of the corporate restaurant. Queuing at the elevators or swinging up the staircase — imitating the Swedes — we were ready to return to our desks.

And there came our manager. A brilliant, graceful but firm, young Swedish woman. Truly a positive personality, esteemed by the whole office. She had taken off her thick jumper. Under her white top she was wearing an extensive, brightly-coloured,

red and green sea life tattoo across her right shoulder and whole upper arm.

She said, 'I encourage you to take a walk in the sun after lunch and breathe some fresh air. The path to the park starts just behind the building. It's really beautiful and the trees are almost blossoming!'

An awkward silence followed. I was taken aback, and so were some of my colleagues judging by their expressions of unconcealed surprise. I could almost hear the voice of managers I had been acquainted with, from a variety of countries, whispering in unison: 'Needless to say, I encourage you not to prolong your lunch break too wildly today, a lot of work is waiting for us, it's going to be a long afternoon.'

But this was not one of those variety of countries. This was Sweden, a place where the call of the wild will never, ever be seen as a fad.

Be

I like to tell Swedes how much I appreciate the positive sides of their society. At a recent networking event, I was introduced to a Swedish leadership consultant and we started chatting about the vitality of the local business environment. As the conversation drifted to the city of Malmö in general, I couldn't resist mentioning that I had recently tried and enjoyed the Swedish tradition of *kallbad* (having a sauna followed by a swim in the sea, all year round) at the nearby *Malmös Kallbadhus*, or *Kallis*, as the locals call it. She mentioned that she used to go there and we found out that we were living in the same neighbourhood. We could have lunch together sometime, maybe explore a potential collaboration.

A week later, she asked if I wanted to meet and discover how we could plan a small joint event. We could maybe seize the opportunity and go for a sauna to talk about it, she said.

Had this happened upon my arrival in Sweden, I would probably have found the offer weird, but not anymore. Instead I was thinking, 'Well, there's a coffee shop next to the sauna, we could sit and write there, if needed.' We didn't make it that far though. We were simply alternating short stays in the sauna with resting on the outer terraces of this Spartan, entirely wooden, beautiful establishment from 1898.

As we were talking about work, many other purposeful conversations were simultaneously happening in this 85 Celsius room with a view on the bay and the Torso. Suddenly an elderly woman wearing a traditional felt hat exclaimed, 'This is not supposed to be a coffee shop, ladies, please behave!' whereupon everyone switched to whispering mode and continued talking.

The facility is separated into a men's and a women's section, but the sauna attendants responsible for continuously charging the heaters with wood are of any gender. They swing into the sauna practically unnoticed, wearing working trousers and long-sleeved *Kallis* jumpers. They charge the heater quickly and leave immediately, without the sound level of the combined conversations in the sauna being even slightly affected. One easily gets used to their seamless passage, as much as one does to moving around the whole area, indoors and outdoors, wearing strictly nothing.

At one point, we were standing near the wooden benches outside the sauna, pausing between two hot sessions, talking. One attendant, a big, young guy carrying a couple of wood chunks, was passing by. To my surprise, my new friend called out to him, and in my eyes, transforming a seamless silhouette into an animated character. 'Excuse me, I have to ask you,' she said, initiating a casual conversation that continued effortlessly for a little while. A naked woman and a fully-dressed man having an ordinary conversation in a public place as if it was not even slightly awkward.

Sweat

Becoming a small business owner has allowed me to get in touch with a variety of people and environments. It brought me, for example, to a free course on accountancy literacy for start-ups. We were a dozen people, hosted by a public entity whose mission it was to support entrepreneurship through a network of local offices.

Our host guided us to a meeting room and we sat down. The presentation was about to start when a last participant rushed into the meeting room, taking her jacket off, sighing. The young woman took a look around, grabbed the closest free chair, then spoke to the assembly of unknown aspiring entrepreneurs and the presenter with a smile, 'Before we start I'd like to take a short moment to regain my composure. I have been cycling here in a rush and I am sweating and sweating, and it's quite hot in here!'

What self-awareness and confidence! In her shoes, I'd probably have headed to the toilets and hidden there for a while, preferring to join the group three minutes late rather than signalling my inadequacy with my sweaty forehead.

Train

Fast forward to the present day. 2017 is coming to an end. Browsing LinkedIn, I stumble on a post written in a rather provocative tone by a Swedish executive of a well-known retail company.

Leaning on research on the health benefits of exercising together with colleagues during working hours, the author was using colourful language to express her astonishment about the lack of this practice in a number of Swedish companies. Arguing that common exercise has been proven to bring extensive benefits at no cost in terms of productivity, the manager was making the case for a generalized active support to such initiatives, pointing out the necessity for the board to lead by example and, in so doing, seize the opportunity to become more familiar with more employees. She concluded by mentioning the specific training practice they had gone for as a company.

On a factual note, this post was extremely successful, getting a whopping 150 000 views, as well as a huge response in terms of comments and likes. In a country of 10 millions, I think one can safely say that the urge expressed in this post definitely hit a nerve.

Connecting Pieces

Is there space for a common trait to emerge here, now that the pieces are in front of us? To me all these pieces connect and tell a foundational story. A story that brushes the elemental role of our physical body in our existence. Every culture has its own way to tell this vital story and it seems to me that the Swedish take on it is one that celebrates acceptance and grounding.

In this country, I feel I've touched what I would call the biological hyper-dignity that our bodies deserve. Our bodies are to be respected and cultivated of course. Still, the matter here is neither vanity, nor anxious performance obsession. There's more.

There's a profoundly ingrained sense of our physical intelligence and dignity that we we can't just pretend doesn't exist because of a professional context, or any other codified social situation. Our bodies are our gateway to experiences, so they have to come first. Just because we are working, it doesn't mean we can pretend some higher reason or obligation suddenly becomes all that matters and our bodies have just vanished.

Invigorating the body wins over administrative distance at the tax office. The health maintenance contribution makes employees feel more engaged, aligned with the corporate values and even more connected with each other. An energizing walk in nature wins over work overload. Even more astonishing, people don't have to lose their usual conversational aptitudes just because they're naked. Sweating wins over shame and exercising together at work is considered a major accomplishment for a whole nation of employees.

Paraphrasing one of Blaise Pascal's well-known aphorisms, here in Sweden it's a given that not only the heart, but the whole body has its reasons that reason does not know. Besides, what easier way to understand equality is there than realising how equal we become as soon as we develop this perception of our body's reason? Hence why so many Swedes enjoy having their directors doing yoga together with all the staff of the company. Equality wins over corporate hierarchy through our bodies, which are never shameful nor worthless to acknowledge.

Looking again at everyday working life, making the body comfortable first has become a basic principle for event planners. It's part of the experience design. No coffee, no success. Offering refreshment for the body is considered the bare minimum, by definition hassle-free and completely free, be it a morning coffee, lunch or even dinner, if applicable.

With this in mind, we easily understand why one of the most popular knowledge and meeting hubs for the high-tech community in Malmö has decided to start their About page like this: 'Foo Café started in Malmö, Sweden. Open both day and evening, we make sure high-quality espresso is always available, together with snacks and cold beer.'

I tend to read the traditional *fika* likewise, as an acknowledgment that we need to purposefully offer our bodies some relief during our workday. We are all the same in this respect — humans in need of resetting our energy levels and taking a moment together, no matter how many dozens of e-mails are waiting for a reply in our inbox.

The body in the Swedish workplace is dignified in many other ways. We have seen, for instance, that sweating is acceptable and not only for professional athletes. Whereas elsewhere it is often associated with inefficiency, unfitness, stress and shame, sweating might be interpreted as a sign of activity and determination in Sweden. One of the major gym chains is called *Friskis o Svettis*, literally 'Healthy and Sweaty'. Would you say such a brand could be a nationwide success in other countries?

Another example is the way Swedes approach looks, outfits and image. More or less intentionally, we all express ourselves through the choices we make about our appearance. Our body is not only our gateway to absorb experiences, but also a language. It channels our message from the inside out, be it an expression of freedom, belonging, allegiance, criticism or other. Allowing our physical presence to be a language for our individual expression, and not only a signal of adaptation and conformity to a given group or situation, is another way to honour the dignity of the body and its reasons.

In Sweden, dressing up is experienced more as a choice than an act of compliance to any code or uniform. There are certainly variations, but in most circumstances anyone can work out a way to be socially and professionally credible, while liberally wearing their preferred combination of styles, items, statement pieces and body upgrades, including cross-body sea life tattoos.

Even one of the most official and symbolic uniforms, the military uniform, is applicable for reinvention, provided that it's done in moderation. That's how Sweden's Armed Forces have recently shown solidarity with the Pride movement by publishing a picture of military boots with rainbow laces.

Another way to prioritize the primary, private and physical life over workplace habits and traditions is workplace mobility. Working from home, at least occasionally, is common, often as a result of a quick, informal arrangement with the employer. In this way, not only the physical body of the individual, but also the family as an organic entity can express and satisfy their needs more flexibly. Swedes are not afraid of being early adopters of this rising global workplace trend. Many employers are ready to experiment and deconstruct the concept of the traditional office, transforming the workplace into a virtual, modular space that employees can access from whatever desk they happen to be sitting at.

I can't resist concluding on a language note. Sometimes mysterious, language is often revealing, as it runs parallel to the cultural mind-set. I was attending a 'train the trainers' seminar for facilitators last month. At lunch, day three, one of the attendees was explaining his understanding of how feelings affect facilitation versus how emotions do. In response, another attendee, a Swede, reflected, 'What's the difference exactly? In Swedish we only have the word *känsla*, meaning emotion and feeling.' 'Well, the word *emotion* does exist,' she continued, 'but only as a concept in social sciences, it's not really used in everyday language.'

It struck me that this language difference is consistent with the Swedish hyper-dignity of the body. What's important is that both feelings and emotions relate to the body. It's of little relevance that feelings originate in the body and then are elaborated on in the mind, while emotions are merely gut feelings. They are both states that we experience, highlighting our intense connection to our physical nature. They both speak the language of our physical intelligence. The rest is poetry or psychological jargon.

Language speculations aside, the Swedish way to apprehend the body has been refreshing and positive in my experience so far. It has invited me to uncover connections with people in an immediate and natural way. At times, it has helped me overcome a tendency to make things too cerebral and intellectual. Because these perceptions are affected by origin, background and personality, one could make sense of similar pieces of experience in quite different ways.

Do you like puzzles? If you do and are a newcomer to Sweden, you're probably going through a shaking rollercoaster phase while staying curious and learning at the same time. Soon a meaningful picture will start emerging. That's how the best puzzles reward curiosity and perseverance.

Without any loud announcement, a subtle sense will make its way into your daily life and start working for you. You will surprise yourself by being able to read and master a new code, no longer feeling like an outsider in your own world. At times you will anticipate situations, even inadvertently behaving in ways your Swedish acquaintances probably would. Your old friends will notice it, affectionately making fun of your latest habits.

Eventually your carefully compiled and researched impression of Sweden will have taken its very unique shape. If you keep on building up your wisdom and growing your confidence until this happens, you will win. Your quest for context and meaning will be fulfilled.

Olga Talalay

Country of origin: Russia.
Profession and current occupation: Finance.
Arrived in Sweden: 2014.
Reason for coming to Sweden: I used the opportunity to move for work to escape the unbearable political regime in Russia.
Reason for staying in Sweden: Same as above, and I discovered the amazing Swedish synth scene.

Untitled

Introduction by the editor

Olga Talalay explores unheeded sources of light in the everyday landscape of commuting between her work and home in Stockholm. Now settled in Sweden, her gaze is no longer that of a tourist or visitor, hurriedly documenting the obvious or sun-lit attractions. Instead she turns towards her routine, the now predictable and mundane. Although this inevitably suggests boredom, there is a sense of security linked to this, a feeling of belonging and trusting that the subjects can be returned to, to be explored again, and in another light.

Veronika Opatřilová

Country of origin: Czech Republic.
Profession: Freelance writer and Stockholm guide.
Current occupation: I'm writing a book and baking cakes for a small café in Brno in my spare time.
Arrived in Sweden: 2012.
Reason for coming to Sweden: I fell in love with Swedish nature, the sound of the language, *fika*, and two Swedish bands, Mando Diao and Sugarplum Fairy.
Other: I write about Sweden for several online magazines such as Routes North, Globuzzer and a Czech blog about Sweden: Sverige.cz. I am also working on a Czech tourist guide book about Stockholm, my second novel and an translation of my first novel called Playlist (Jack Franz).

A departure is the arrival to someplace new

I lived many different lives during that one life I spent in Sweden. I was that easily-missed, imperceptible cleaner in your homes; the one that came early in the morning and owned the keys to your houses, the one you had never really seen, yet knew all of your secrets, every minor detail of your life.

I was the smiling girl behind the desk at that coffee place close to your favourite amusement park; the one that brought you the plate of *gravad lax* and whose accent you couldn't decipher, you were wondering until you forgot about her completely.

I was the one that taught your precious children Spanish; you might have met me once at the door while coming home from your highly prestigious work. I helped your beloved children to get better marks in a subject they didn't care about. I was from some unknown eastern country and, after the New Year, you didn't bother to answer my e-mails anymore because I wasn't a native speaker after all and you weren't sure what language impact I would have on your children.

I was the one you could use for a temporary research job in my mother tongue, since no one else in Gothenburg spoke that weird language. I was the one preparing your hamburger with chips behind the desk at the fast food restaurant during the break in your favourite concert or football game, when you got up from your seat to buy a beer and something unhealthy to eat.

It was me who prepared you the perfectly cooked piece of beef. I was the one whose article about Stockholm you might have read on the internet. It was me who welcomed you at the harbour when you arrived on those expensive, huge cruise ships, who took you through the beautiful city of Stockholm and told you all those stories and facts about Sweden, who laughed with you over a cup of coffee and then hugged you goodbye before you disappeared forever.

It was me, Vicky. Living the life I dreamt about so much it hurt. It was me trying to be one of you, trying to fit in. It was me trying to live the simple and happy life. I did my best. But I didn't know that Sweden was a heartless guy that breaks your heart without knowing about it or meaning to. Charming, so easy-going, so fascinating and completely cold. It didn't really matter how hard I tried, I couldn't force Sweden to love me.

I tried to figure out what I did wrong. I had various theories about this love of my life. I blamed my name that sounded too eastern and exotic. I blamed my Czech accent that sometimes made Swedish people think I was Finnish. I blamed my degree in Spanish language and literature, who cares about that up north. I blamed my choices and I blamed Sweden for not wanting me enough. Until I stopped blaming, quit trying and let go of the illusion we were meant to be together.

One life, just one, yet I lived through so many different stories. Concepts about life I lost, universal truths I learned to question, all the perspectives I gained. From the sex toys you left on your unmade beds when I entered your houses and cleaned the toilets you forgot to flush. I dusted the little wooden *dalahästar* you put on the window sills in the beautiful kitchens you never really used because of the lack of time. I smelled the microwaved food you cooked after your well-paid jobs. I touched the fancy clothes in your wardrobes, looked from your windows over Rålambshovsparken to the streets of Kungsholmen. I dreamt about being you. I understood so much about you through the stories of your children, told in broken Spanish. I saw you through the many different eyes of all the world nationalities that had ever crossed the borders of Sweden and spent a few hours with me exploring the city of lakes spread over 14 islands.

But it was just me all the time; loving Sweden with every inch of my soul, so unconditionally. And all I wanted was to stay. I never gave up on you Sweden. Even after I came back, I searched for you in every corner of my little country whose name you never understood. You who had so often drunk so much cheap beer in Prague; you never knew where my country lay, what my language sounded like, you never understood why I came and you always wondered when I would go back; until I did.

From the moment I stood at the rainy railway station in Malmö in 2012, I changed like a chameleon every month just to please you, just for you to allow me to stay.

It wasn't until I left the country behind me that I blissfully blurred into the Swedish reality. I finally got the job I had always dreamt of. The one with the regular pay check, the one from 8 a.m. to 4.30 p.m. The one that allowed me a decent existence, a two-room apartment and meal vouchers every month. Only at night I dreamt of the Baltic Sea. In those dreams, for a perplexing reason I couldn't understand, I was frantically crying.

Here, 2500 km from my dream life, begins my real Swedish career. Don't be surprised if I call you one day, and said 'My name´s Vicky and I am calling you from *Elgiganten*' and it would really be me. The same me as before. The one you wouldn't even consider inviting for a job interview for the position of the customer support agent. I speak Swedish eight hours every day. I call you in Swedish to tell you that your newly-bought electronic item will be delayed. I left your country just to find a piece of it in the place I call home. And every day, when nobody is watching, I am travelling through all those well-known places on Google maps, each number I dial is one piece of my Swedish story. My accent suddenly is no hindrance at all. Nor is my name.

During all these lives I was both invisible and the centre of attention; I was lost, but also found the utmost happiness. No matter what I did, this Swedish career of mine waited for me outside the Swedish borders, silently waiting for me to come, without me knowing that my failure in Sweden was my win somewhere else.

6. Belonging

In a new culture, we become acutely aware of the practices, beliefs and values we have – or don't have – in common with those around us. Being part of that new group inevitably makes us question cultural attributes that we have previously taken for granted, meaning that we are changing, adapting, growing – shrinking. Perhaps we are less of the independent individual we think of ourselves to be, and more of just another piece of something much bigger.

Our sense of belonging and identity may also be challenged when returning to what we have left behind. Alienated from our past but not yet being comfortable with our role in the present, our sense of belonging is a pursuit that, per definition, will take us further and further away from the answer we are looking for.

Simplicity and humility
Nausherwan Ghaffar

Perhaps because I have become a vegetarian
Angeliki Vlachou

A Mexican dreamer in corporate Sweden
Marco Guadarrama

6

Nausherwan Ghaffar

Country of origin: Pakistan.
Profession and occupation: Operation manager (sales).
Arrived in Sweden: 2009.
Reason for coming to Sweden: I came to Sweden to pursue a master's program at Uppsala University.
Reason for staying in Sweden: I got a great opportunity to work at a prestigious management consulting firm in Stockholm and also, having lived in Sweden for two years by then, I had, more or less, fallen in love with it.

Simplicity and humility

One of the richest men in Sweden walked into our office. When I say rich, I am talking billions of dollars rich. The gentleman, who had walked in, heads one of Sweden's most iconic corporations. Not surprisingly, he was one of Sweden's most well-known business personalities. He signed in at the reception and asked to see one of our senior partners. He just stood there, waiting for someone to show up and collect him. He stood there, just like any other visitor to the office would.

Just a few metres away, I stood with a few of my colleagues waiting to try the new coffee machine. I was in complete awe of the corporate legend who had just walked in. My colleagues however, all of whom were Swedes, seemed completely aloof from what was happening. They couldn't wait to fill their cups. As soon as they had done that, they were on their way to their desks, just like they would be on any other day.

That, to sum up, is why I love my adopted homeland. If there's one word that comes to my mind when I think of professional culture here, its 'humility'. If you'd push me to come up with a second word, that would be 'simplicity'. I've been living in Sweden for almost nine years now and I am still amazed at how the cultural values here refuse to glorify wealth or power. My colleagues knew very well who the gentleman waiting at the reception was. He had one of the most familiar profiles when it came to the financial press. He'd have his picture on one of the main pages, if not the front page, of *Dagens Industri* (Sweden's premier business daily) once a week at least. To my colleagues, however, he was the same as anyone else who'd walk in for an appointment. He wasn't worthy of any special welcome. He was just someone, waiting to be collected. That was it.

Throughout the time I have spent in Sweden, I have regularly been reminded of these traits that exist within Swedish society in general, and Sweden's professional culture specifically. No one seems to be concerned with what you're wearing, e.g. whether you're wearing a brand new high-end designer suit or a second-hand one. I know people who could afford not one but multiple luxury sports cars, but who prefer taking the subway to work every morning or even take their bike, when convenient. I also know people who could dump their broken smartphones and get new ones, just for the fun of it, yet they enjoy fixing their broken phones themselves.

Back in Pakistan, where I am from, things run on a different track. Flaunting seems to be the thing there. If you were Pakistan's equivalent of the office guest waiting at the reception, you could (without exaggeration) expect a red carpet welcome wherever you went, with people lined up to shake your hand. You might even get a red carpet farewell (if there is such a thing) just for showing up at some event for a few minutes. You'd show up in a high-end luxury sedan or an SUV wherever you'd go — even if you're passing through the narrowest, dingiest streets imaginable where the sheer width of your ride is an inconvenience rather than a luxury. You'd be throwing lavish parties for high-ranking bureaucrats and officials and showering them with take-home gifts, just to have the way cleared in case a new government would come in.

Having been born and brought up in Pakistan, I had (prior to arriving in Sweden) developed this notion that the ability to flaunt wealth and power is, as disgusting as it may sound, something to strive for. It's what I grew up with and it's what I thought was right, unfortunately. Living and, more significantly, working here opened my eyes. Our wealth, our possessions, our spending patterns and our material excesses should not be our defining traits. The realisation that my happiness is not contingent upon winning the 'rat race' is one of the most beautiful things Sweden has given me. It's something that I, hopefully, will always remember.

Another thing that impresses me time and time again is how flat professional hierarchies are here in Sweden. I have always been encouraged to speak my mind throughout my professional life here. As long as you have substance behind your stance, people will listen. They might have ten years more experience than you and be recognized experts in their respective fields. They might even be someone you directly report to. Speaking your mind is strongly encouraged here. I, for example, have, on numerous occasions, had disagreements with my manager/s, but it has always been amicable and has always ended up in a healthy compromise, with one side compromising more than the other but still, without any hard feelings. Furthermore, there's no insistence on face time and, at least in my experience, you can work from home all you want (depending on your role of course), as long as you're achieving results.

I don't know if I'll have to leave Sweden at some point in time. I might stay. I might not. If I leave, however, my biggest fear is that settling into professional life in some other land, will be a huge challenge. Sweden, through those two cornerstones of 'humility' and 'simplicity' have set the bar very high indeed.

This may be a cold, dark country where the common perception is that it's hard to make friends and build a social life, yet working here has made me realise something far more significant than anything else. It has made me realise that I am much more than what I earn, own and wear. It has made me realise that I should be able to express my thoughts and encourage others to do the same. Most importantly, it has made me realise that life is not a race and I am not competing with anyone.

Those two-three minutes of waiting for my turn to get some coffee taught me an amazing lesson, i.e. that respectable gentleman may have been exceptionally wealthy and extremely influential, but he was also just a visitor waiting to be collected. It's something I'll never forget. Those two-three minutes were beautiful, profound and fulfilling.

Angeliki Vlachou

Country of origin: Greece.
Profession and occupation: Architect.
Arrived in Sweden: 2011.
Reason for coming to Sweden: Study and work.
Reason for staying in Sweden: I stayed because I didn't want to go back to Greece.

Perhaps because I have become a vegetarian

Translated from the Swedish by Sofi Tegsveden Deveaux

Sweden, Stockholm, Högdalen, my own living room. I'm listening to Pink Floyd and it is Christmas Day, 2017. A gloomy day and it has been raining for three days. I am becoming impatient, longing for snow and its silence. This time of the year is peculiar. I know some people suffer from anxiety related to Christmas, either because of them having to spend the holidays alone, or because they didn't have the time to buy gifts for some distant relative of theirs. The first one I can understand and relate to. But although there are plenty of theories about the psychology of Christmas, I fail to understand the hype. Perhaps this is because of where I come from, people worry about other things than how to find time for frenetic Christmas shopping.

On my balcony, a great tit, one of those unremarkable but cute and friendly birds that I have learnt to recognise, is enjoying the fat ball I left out. Beyond, my neighbour is moving her last pot plants into her flat. I let my eyes wander over the tower blocks of Högdalen, and I recall a Swedish the song by Leif Nylén called *Törnrosa* (Sleeping Beauty): '*Fåglarna flög, häcken växte hög, hög som ett höghus i Hässelby gård*' (The birds flew, the hedge grew high, as high as a tower block in Hässelby gård). I have never really been attracted to tall buildings, but there is something appealing about them from a social and architectural point of view. In my mind, they are capsules where people are stored to live, fight their fears and love each other. These days, I am one of those people, in a decrepit suburban tower block, and there is something liberating about this. I am not talking about standing on the rooftop and looking out over the city. There is something else, something about the social history of these buildings that I can't let go of. To me, these buildings, my building, is a symbol for the continuance of the welfare state and the freedom it has meant to the people.

My first encounter with this welfare state, Sweden, was an overcast and wet day in July 2011. It was raining heavily, so I was lucky to be picked up by my new landlady. At the airport, I walked up to her and tried to greet her with a kiss on her cheek, but she politely declined. Apparently, this was not the custom here. The first 15 minutes in the car or so, we sat silently without exchanging any other word than 'Thank you'. Much later, as we were approaching her house, she started speaking.

She told me about the rain that hadn't stopped for three days. This was my first encounter with a Swede — a careful woman who enjoyed talking about the weather.

The first place I lived in was a two-storey, semi-detached house in Åkersberga, 30 km north of Stockholm. I was one of two tenants and my room was on the ground floor. The house was located in the middle of the forest, and my most frequent guests were deer, foxes and squirrels. I was so disappointed one day when I learnt that my landlady didn't share my passion for feeding such beautiful creatures — she made it clear that I had to discontinue this habit.

It took a long time before I felt comfortable with the area, or rather the fact that I lived there, in the middle of a forest. Up until then, I had always lived in a city. The sound of cars honking, drivers swearing at each other, or a short morning chat with the neighbour had been a natural part of my everyday life. But in my new home, everything was different. Through my window, I looked out on birches, pines and firs. My door opened directly on unspoiled nature — or 'spinach', as the Swedes call it. My first impression of this, the city of Stockholm, was awe. I was stunned by the greenery, the lushness. At the same time, I was filled with fear about the new situation I found myself in.

Fear can do so much to people. The reason I moved to a new country was to avoid the limbo of unemployment. At the time

I arrived in Sweden, Greece was a popular subject in the news. It was impossible to avoid questions such as: 'Is it true that people retire in their forties? Why do you guys want to borrow more money again,' and the worst one, not a question but a statement: 'It is not true that Greeks are struggling, I was there last summer and everyone was sunbathing and having coffee.'

During my first months in Sweden, my biggest burden was being Greek. Like most Greeks, I did feel the guilt. Not long before, Theodoras Pangalos, our minister of finance, had made a statement and said: 'We all have the same responsibility for the dept.'

//

Three months passed. I was still in the house in the forest. One usual Svensson Saturday, I woke up to the voices of children playing upstairs. I felt the need to get out as soon as possible, so I took a walk to the local town centre. I was in a good mood and wanted to enjoy the season with all my senses. Autumn had just begun and the beauty of nature was fragile. I could smell the rain from earlier, snails crawled by my feet. For once, I allowed myself to enjoy the moment, paying attention to the little details around me. I felt calm and at ease, very different from my usual journey into town: walking to the bus stop, taking a bus to the centre, and then the train to Stockholm Östra. Most days, I swore and cursed the three hour journey to school and back.

As I finally arrived to my usual destination, I needed to take money out of the cash machine, and queued up. Behind me stood an elderly couple. They were impatient and kept bumping into me. At some point, I had had enough and turned around to look at them. 'Go back to where you came from if you don't like it!' I had been taking Swedish classes for a week and there was no way I could reply. But I did understand. My day was ruined. I felt humiliated, scared, small, hurt. This was perhaps a small thing, but it made me seriously consider the options of returning to Greece. I thought it was pointless to stay if I was unable to feel welcome. But racism is, unfortunately, without borders. Just like love. I stood up, wiped of the dirt, and continued.

//

A few months later, I was able to read Theodor Kallifatides in Swedish, '*Ett nytt land utanför mitt fönster*' (A new country outside my window). I was touched by his experiences and felt less lonely. One sentence stuck with me. '*Jag kunde inte bli kvitt hans blick som fäste sig på mig som en fästing. Det var lika obehagligt att dra ut den som att låta den vara kvar.*' (I couldn't rid myself of his gaze, sticking to me like a tick. It was as disagreeable to pull it out as letting it stay.)

//

Now this is almost seven years ago. Who would have believed that I would have made it all the way here? I doubted, and I doubted for a long time. Would I ever learn the language? Would I find a job as an architect? Would I make new friends? I knew one thing, if I managed to learn the language, I would be able to get a job. A job would mean new people, and probably friends.

In reality it wasn't that easy. Language, work, social belonging. These were three aspects tied together and turning in my head, day and night. I wasn't feeling well, and went through an unbearable life crisis turning into depression, not so much because of the new life, but because of the old one. I pushed myself too much, mistaking anxiety for a driving force and curiosity. But this is not healthy, when anxiety takes over curiosity, things start to get serious.

//

When meeting new people here, the question I hear the most is 'Why did you come to this place in particular? Why did you leave Greece? It was so beautiful that summer on Crete.' I fail to understand how some people can't make a distinction between going on holiday and emigrating. They also ask me why I picked Sweden as 'destination'. Maybe this is their only reference. If you are bored, you pack your bag and leave, to test some new 'destination'. It took me a long time to understand that people mean well. Or at least, I can now remind myself that they mean well. Such a question can be very sensitive for a person who has emigrated. If you have chosen to move in order to maintain your human dignity, this question can seem superficial. It seems like you can't understand that someone could make the decision to move to a new country based on the impossibility of leading a dignified life in your their country. Is this because they never experienced anything like that themselves?

This was the reality for most of my friends at university in Stockholm. When I got to know them, I got the impression that these people never worried. Neither their finances nor their chances of finding a job after graduation seemed to be an issue. Their families were middle-class or upper middle-class. They were all cool and relaxed. They always had stories to share, stories from travelling after graduation from school and before starting university. Taking a sabbatical like this is quite common in Sweden, and not just for young people. You travel around for a year, collecting experiences, seeing new places and meeting new people. You give yourself some time to contemplate your interests, skills and future.

This sounds like a brilliant idea, but before I came to Sweden, completely foreign to me. The thought of travelling around for a year — just for the sake of travelling — had never crossed my mind. I could never afford trips just for the fun of it, and I worked hard to not have to be financially dependent on my parents. In Greece, your parents pay your rent if you study somewhere other than your hometown. As there are no student grants, you have to take part-time work — shit work, to make ends meet. This whole thing prevented me from feeling relaxed as a student — or rather, as a human being. It was such a strain to finish my studies without delays, as my parents would never be able to help me. Although my parents never explicitly said so, I knew they were struggling. It was my duty to work hard and be productive.

This feeling of duty has followed me my whole adult life, and this was maybe the one thing that made it impossible for me to identify with other students. I was there, in a foreign country, with a budget strictly limited to two years — this was the length of my master's programme. I strived, all on my own, for a safe and quiet future. They were here, with a different family background, student grants and student flats. For someone from another part of Sweden, the worst thing that could happen was the prospect of having to stay with a relative in Stockholm. I remember one particular girl who was so annoyed because she had to share a two-bedroom flat with her single aunt who lived in Farsta.

I felt inferior and spent a lot of time on my own. I had no privileges that I could take for granted. Perhaps I need to emphasize that the reason I am writing this is not to get sympathy, but a belief in sharing your life experiences. I have seen quite a bit now, and although my life in Sweden has — so far — been relatively successful, I know very well that others have been, and will be, in the same situation.

When the first academic year ended, most of my fellow students started internships at the municipalities or architectural practices. This was supposed to prepare them for real work upon graduation a year later. Despite having studied Swedish for nine months and the fact that I could communicate in a basic manner, I didn't manage to get myself an internship.

The number of rejection letters I received was high, but there were even more applications that were never answered. I wrote back to the nice ones, that ones that took their time to reject me, to ask the simple question: on what grounds they based their decision. Only one person replied and the answer was that I didn't seem to have mastered the Swedish language. Sure I hadn't. But I was able to communicate. Despite all my grammatical errors. At this point, my despair turned into rage. And rage into courage. I asked my landlady at the time if I could do an internship at her husband's welder workshop. Of course, they said no. But from then on, my luck turned. I joined a Facebook group for people living in Åkersberga, where I wrote a short post saying that I could help with anything from taking care of children or animals, to cleaning or gardening. Most people wanted a cleaner.

As it turned out, I ended up taking care of a six-year-old autistic girl that summer. This small, disabled girl was the first person who could actually understand what I was saying in my new language. And I had finally landed my first job in Sweden. I was so proud of myself. Through this position, I also got my first insights into Swedish family life. A single mother with a well-paid job, but a lot on her mind. She rarely managed to care properly for her child. She was very direct and open about her experiences — that her life was falling apart and she just wanted to get away from everything. I appreciated that she was so direct and dared to talk about this with me, but I also had the impression that I primarily filled the function of a psychologist. Several times she came to me to ask how to handle one situation or another. I took this as an invitation to suggest concrete solutions. For example, I advised her to send her girl to another school, and to reduce her medication, as what the girl needed more than anything else was a present mother. But her reaction was unexpected, and I was told that I was nosy and lacked respect. This was a sad ending, but I learnt a lot from this experience. It was the first time I got to know a Swede on a deeper level.

//

I tried some different jobs throughout the years, before finding the first one that I could describe as satisfying — my current employment, and the fourth one as an architect. I worked as a housekeeper for a rich family living on Karlaplan, as a cleaner for upper middle-class families in Hornstull and Danderyd, and other households while employed by a big cleaning company. I helped a spoiled 15-year-old with their homework, I sold strawberries, watched dogs (and cats) and functioned as a nanny for two cute little sisters in Hammarby Sjöstad. I also did some measuring work for Statistics Sweden, counting the number of passengers at the bus terminal at Slussen, on a -20 Celsius day.

During my time as a housekeeper with the family on Karlaplan, I experienced immeasurable frustration. Three people shared an enormous flat from the early 20th century, with six bedrooms and a total of 270 square metres. The woman had a high position within the culture sector and the man had an executive position at a bank. They were still not happy with their lives. She escaped through self-harming behaviour and was clearly an alcoholic. He was probably going through some age-related crisis and was trying to prove he was an attractive alpha male by having several mistresses. The child, a girl, was eight years old and she was the saddest, most spoiled and self-obsessed child I have ever met. One day, she came back from school and couldn't find her phone. My job was to search the whole flat, but I couldn't find it. Three days later the mother texted me and said I couldn't continue working for them. This event still comes back to me. I am now almost certain that she believed I was responsible for the lost phone.

/ /

I started my first job as an architect nine months after graduation. It was an internship — decently paid — at a small architectural practice. My boss was a nice man from the north of Sweden and I also had a colleague from Denmark. Yes, my willingness to escape being a foreigner was great enough for me to understand a Dane speaking with a southern Swedish accent. But one day I overheard a consultant asking my boss if he could actually understand my Swedish. I don't know if he said so intending for me to hear it, or if he believed I wouldn't understand. The question remains.

When the internship ended, I continued to look for jobs in architecture, but I had to take another job in the meantime. I ended up working as a personal assistant for three different people with dementia and cerebral palsy. I changed schools and started learning Swedish at *ABF*. At this time, I spoke to another student in my class, who was a Spanish teacher, and who had recently built a house built with a turnkey enterprise. They needed help from an architect, apparently. And I got a job there, on a 75% basis, not working Fridays. It was good until I was told off for asking about holiday allowance. This was my second job as an architect and I needed the experience for my CV, so I put up with my boss anyway. But, frankly, she was nothing but a capitalist witch who exploited her power position and wanted to humiliate me as soon as she had the chance. I resigned after one year's 'collaboration'.

I have met all types of people and have experienced both pleasant and unpleasant circumstances. I have been asked to stay silent about things I overheard. I have seen unfaithful couples lying to each other. Parents parking their children in front of the TV. I have been bitten by a small and spoiled dog — you know the type, barking at everything. I had to work eight hours without going to the bathroom as 'the clients need to know someone is around'. I have also been very humiliated. It is curious how managers behave like swines just because they can. One thing I learnt is not to apologise too much. You can and should stand up for yourself if you want to be seen, at the same time as being kind and approachable of course. But I keep reminding myself that no fight has been won if I have only been nice.

//

The officer who took care of me at the unemployment agency once told me that you have to try out different jobs until you find the dream job. She was right. It's not true that you will find your dream job just because you are good at what you are doing and really want something. Recently, I listened to a radio interview with the new party leader of *Moderaterna*, who claimed that Sweden is no Downtown Abbey and that we are not living in early 20th century England. He said we shouldn't be held back by an old-fashioned order where, for example, all welders should remain welders, imprisoned by gender, class or clan. He concluded 'What you want is what you do'. I am so upset by this attitude, so prominent in the party of *Moderaterna*. Most political parties see social mobility as a carrot in front of the citizen. Such an invented term, social mobility.

Every time I return to my parents' home, I feel confused. I feel I can't reconcile my different identities. Coming from a lower middle-class family in Greece (being the equivalent of Swedish working class) and now belonging to the Swedish middle class, feels like I'm lost. A sad past, a successful present. My mind turns chaotic when I think about the latter being a result of the former. This journey would have been impossible without leaving family and friends behind. During my first years in Sweden this estrangement was so marked that I had to re-define myself. Due to this, my old relationships changed and became so distorted that I judged them to be inferior to the new ones. Perhaps because I belong to the first generation to get their degrees after the political shift in the 1970's. Perhaps financially. Perhaps because I have become a vegetarian.

//

After some time in Sweden, I struggled with the idea of having to speak Greek with my co-patriots if there were any Swedes present. I told myself that it was impolite to use a language not everyone could understand. But the main reason was that I didn't want to stand out as a foreigner. I have now concluded that this limitation I set myself was deeply racist, and I have stopped it. Now, if I find a Greek person, I chatter away in Greek regardless of any Swede being present. Why? The bitter explanation is that I am now beyond my fears. Language, work, social belonging, as I mentioned earlier, no longer scare me. I know the language, I have a job and I live together with a Swede. So, well, I am now relatively well off and have the right to speak Greek without censoring myself. Sad but true.

Sad because I have turned down some Greeks I could have been friends with. In their eyes, I was turning into a stranger, but what was happening was that I was fighting not to be a stranger in the eyes of Swedes.

//

I have seen a lot in my life, and come far from where I started, but I can't rid myself of the heavy burden of homesickness. I have made friends with strangers and have become familiar with bizarre situations, but I know I'm like that song, 'dust in the wind'. Swirling, looking for somewhere to land. I would like to see my own crossing of the class divide as beyond stereotypes or preconceived opinions about success against all odds, and as a proof that meritocracy works as societal construction. Like the American dream; just a fiction that anyone from any background could reach any position in society. I would like to rid myself of my feelings of guilt, related to be regarded as superior to others in my home country, at the same time as I'm not good enough in Sweden. At the same time, I need to recognise that the vital parts of my true self are still there — I am the person I always was. And yes, social mobility is like the songs of sirens. Now, here, I have learnt that the opportunity to change class is something that an unequal society promises people in order for them not to ask for equality for all.

//

The rain has calmed down. I change Pink Floyd for Jan Johansson, *Jazz på svenska*. Outside, the rain has turned into fog that is encapsulating the buildings, suffocating its victims to sleep. The cat is dozing in her bed — she has travelled all the way from Greece to here, and so have I. This text is my personal mythology and it helps me face the invisible loneliness that comes with always being a stranger. It is important for me to be aware of who I was when I arrived here. To remember who I have been helps me to continue being what I have become.

A life in a cold country is like an onion — the different layers don't only keep you warm, but also together. And when summer comes, the innermost sprout wants to shoot its leaves and shout that life is still here. That is why it releases vapour when being chopped, bringing tears to my eyes. Karin Boye agrees: Yes. Of course. It hurts.

Marco Guadarrama

Country of origin: Mexico.
Profession: Design strategist.
Current occupation: Creative innovator at IKEA of Sweden.
Arrived in Sweden: 2015.
Reason for coming to Sweden: I wanted to experience Scandinavian living.
Reason for staying in Sweden: Human development.
Other: I believe that everything is possible.

A Mexican dreamer in corporate Sweden

'We will not tell you what you've done wrong, but rather make sure you will hear what you've done right.' This was the first advice I received when I moved to Sweden to start working at the well-known Swedish furniture giant. According to this philosophy, the ability to identify and work to rectify one's mistakes is the responsibility of every employee, and is imperative for growth, for both the individual and the company. However, being aware of one's mistakes is not an easy task. Especially as an expat in Sweden.

My first year living here, I focused on work. I felt a big responsibility to fulfil the expectations of the company who had given me this life-changing opportunity. My efforts seemed validated — I was consistently told that I was doing a good job. 'Am I really doing a good job or is everyone trying to build up my confidence,' I asked my manager. He replied, cryptically (to me), 'Neither the best nor the worst is expected from you, but only good enough — *lagom*,' meaning — not too much, not too little, but just right.

What I came to realise was that trying to over-deliver, stand out or achieve more than others is not praised in Sweden. It's more about equality of results. If your colleagues are not suggesting that you do something differently, it means you are on the right track. The most talented and experienced spend their time helping those less capable so that everyone ends up being average. Work teams are structured this way, sharing the same space and resources, so that all units can learn from one another and grow at the same pace. If you try to stand out, the workforce and society as a whole will remind you that good enough is enough.

This philosophy is very different from my previous experiences working in Japan and the United States, where competition is fierce and there's a real fear of falling behind — or getting judged — if you don't exceed expectations, which is usually done by working longer hours. Swedes are conscious about others (and their own) well-being. After 4 p.m. most people are at home enjoying themselves with their families.

In Swedish work culture, building relationships is essential for the success of any project. However, I find there are few opportunities to interact with co-workers outside the office. Many Swedes draw a distinct line between work and their private lives. Casual conversations at work happen mostly over *fika*: a short break during working hours in which we enjoy coffee and cookies together while talking mostly about the weather.

Without clearly-framed activities (organised events with a clear purpose like working, sport activities, classes, lectures, etc.), it's hard to interact with others. People in Sweden live their lives at home, safe from the weather and from uncomfortable human interactions. Booking dinner with co-workers could take months of planning. However, spending time with colleagues outside the office has always been a fantastic and refreshing experience. People usually wait for the sporadic after-work reunions to share their ideas a bit more openly and relaxed. It has been during those moments that I have been able to get better feedback from my colleagues and laugh together. I got to know a soft side of Swedes that you cannot see at first sight.

In Sweden, companies are essentially democratic. There is an absence of strong hierarchies and it's not easy to identify what the roles and responsibilities of employees are. People dress casually, work together and take decisions as a group. It's important that everyone has the opportunity to express their opinion in order to prevent tension. Swedish people avoid confrontation by all means. In order to move forward, it's necessary to reach a consensus, even when it takes longer. This might seem inefficient and drawn out, but ultimately decisions can be reached rather quickly in such flat organisations.

People far down the chain of command are empowered to take action and the decision-making process can ultimately be quite efficient.

In such a flat organisations, I struggled to understand – what does leadership look like? I once asked the business leader of my unit this question. 'I like to lead the way I used to ski,' he told us (he used to be a ski trainer). He continued, 'I made sure everyone had all the equipment they needed, I shared basic instructions and then we just skied together. I avoided telling people what to do or not to do. However, I made sure I was visible and reachable at all times. In this way we could all enjoy the mountain.' In Sweden, leadership is more about credibility and visibility than expertise. Being an expert in Sweden can only take you so far. Trust and inclusion are key characteristics of a successful leader.

Swedish corporate culture is not easy to navigate. Working as an expat in Sweden is full of challenges and misunderstandings. Being polite, for example, is highly culturally biased. Swedes try so hard to not disturb others that it leads to situations where they simply ignore people and their surroundings and, as a consequence, appear rude to expats. Understanding the Swedish idea of harmony is very complex and abstract. As expats, when in fear and doubt, we should focus on the positive, of which there is an abundance in Sweden.

After three years living in Sweden, I feel that I have just started to scratch the surface of what it means to be part of this workforce. The long winters and being far away from the people we call family allows for a lot of reflection and self-criticism. It's common to feel lonely and misunderstood. But in order to cope with the cultural clash, one must be patient and stay curious. Sooner or later, the sun always comes to Sweden, and with it lots of happiness and fulfilment.

My Swedish career has made me question my own behaviour, but this has, ultimately, led to my own human development and professional growth. I've been observing and learning as much as I can from Swedish people and culture while staying authentic and true to myself — a dreamer from Mexico City.

Companies need to explore and understand the value of a wider range of people and learn from the failures and successes of others. As foreigners coming to work in Sweden, we contribute by bringing different perspectives on existing Swedish processes and philosophies. We work to inspire and bring energy to each other. As a result, as I was told at the beginning of my journey in Sweden, both the company and the employee evolve together. *Tillsammans!*

Sofi Tegsveden Deveaux
Editor

Country of origin: Sweden.
Profession: Swedish language teacher, cultural trainer, co-founder of Bee Swedish.
Current occupation: I help internationals settling in Sweden.
Returned to Sweden: 2008.
Reason for returning to Sweden: After seven years abroad I was incredibly homesick for swimming in black forest lakes and walking barefoot on pine needles.
Other: Co-author of *Working in Sweden – The A–Z Guide,* an introductory handbook for international professionals in Sweden.

Lightning Source UK Ltd.
Milton Keynes UK
UKHW021832060120
356473UK00018B/752/P

9 789198 471595